Canada's Most Notorious Serial Killers

Jack Smith

Copyrights

All rights reserved. © Jack Smith (2017) and Maplewood Publishing (2017). No part of this publication or the information in it may be quoted from or reproduced in any form by means such as printing, scanning, photocopying, or otherwise without prior written permission of the copyright holder.

Disclaimer and Terms of Use

Effort has been made to ensure that the information in this book is accurate and complete. However, the author and the publisher do not warrant the accuracy of the information, text, and graphics contained within the book due to the rapidly changing nature of science, research, known and unknown facts, and internet. The author and the publisher do not hold any responsibility for errors, omissions, or contrary interpretation of the subject matter herein. This book is presented solely for motivational and informational purposes only.

Warning

Throughout the book there are some descriptions of murders and crime scenes that some people might find disturbing. There are also language used by people involved in the murders that may not be appropriate.

ISBN: 978-1725893825

Printed in the United States

Contents

The Most Notorious Murderers _____ 1

of the Maple Leaf _____ 1

Robert Pickton The Pigheaded Killer _____ 3

Russell Williams Trouble in Trenton _____ 21

Bruce McArthur Stalking Toronto's Village _____ 37

Paul Bernardo The Scarborough Rapist _____ 67

Clifford Olson The Beast of British Columbia _____ 79

Cody Legebokoff The Country Boy Killer _____ 89

Allan Joseph Legere The Monster of the Miramichi _____ 101

Gilbert Paul Jordan The Boozing Barber _____ 113

Canada's Most Notorious Serial Killers _____ 127

Further Readings _____ 129

Also by Jack Smith _____ 133

The Most Notorious Murderers of the Maple Leaf

Canada, the Northern neighbor of the United States, is best known for its friendly sensibility, cold winters, and hockey games. When people think about Canada, they don't generally think about serial killings. But the U.S. and Mexico aren't the only North American countries that serial killers have called home: All throughout its centuries-long history, Canada has had its own fair share of murderous maniacs.

This book presents accounts of eight of the worst serial killers to tread Canadian soil in recent memory.

Robert Pickton
The Pigheaded Killer

Picking on Pickton

Robert "Willie" Pickton was born on October 24, 1949, on his family's pig farm in Port Coquitlam, British Columbia. His life was difficult from the very beginning; it is said that he came into this world with his umbilical cord tightly wound around his throat, deprived of precious oxygen while the midwife struggled to cut him free.

His parents sometimes speculated that this trauma had caused learning disabilities and possibly irreversible brain damage as well. His defense team likewise latched onto this angle many years later, producing an IQ test which supposedly indicated rather low intelligence. But even if Pickton wasn't a genius—even if he actually did suffer from brain damage—no one could say he wasn't a resilient young man.

He grew up in some rather difficult straits. The rustic farm his parents called home often didn't have running water, and Pickton's earliest memory was of being a toddler lifting up the floorboard under his bed to gain access to the fresh spring water that flowed underneath. In this demanding environment, Robert Pickton apparently became a self-starter who learned and did things at a much younger age than most—including driving the family truck at the age of three.

As Pickton tells the story, he was left by himself in his dad's vintage Maple Leaf truck, a Canadian/General Motors classic from the 1940s. He excitedly jumped into the driver's seat and accidentally knocked the vehicle into neutral. The truck lurched forward and pigs went flying as it careened down the sloping terrain before the panicked young Pickton steered the truck right into a telephone pole. After he was pulled from the wrecked truck, his father "beat the hell" out of him. His dad apparently wasn't mad that he'd been playing around, or even driving the truck—he was just mad that he'd crashed it!

It seems that Pickton's mother and father took an unusual approach to raise children in general. Just a year after this incident, his mother caught him smoking a cigarette—and her way of curing him of this bad habit was to hand him a cigar! Yes, that's right, she had her four-year-old son cram a stogie down his throat and forced him to smoke himself sick. Admittedly, it worked; Pickton never wanted to smoke again.

The days of Robert Pickton's youth unfolded long before Child Protective Services began swooping down on the slightest aberration in childcare. With no outside authority keeping watch, Pickton was completely at the mercy of the oddball parenting practiced by his mother and father, Leonard and Louise.

It was the extreme oddity of Louise Pickton in particular that locals would remember most clearly, many years after the fact. She was decidedly unhygienic in her habits, with a mouth full of rotten teeth, a head that was almost completely bald (except for a few mousy strands covered by a bandanna), and a face with a fuzzy beard sprouting from its surface. Apparently not caring a whit how she looked, Louise would boldly trot out of the house in a dress and boots, screaming at the top of her lungs to Robert and his siblings, "Git over here—now!!"

Robert was his mother's main target, and she was constantly berating him and ordering him around. His father, a Briton who had moved to Canada as a young man, was more distant in his parenting style, usually choosing to remain aloof.

Life was hard on the Picktons' pig farm. The kids were constantly busy cleaning up after the animals, which included a handful of cows as well as over 200 pigs. Pig farms, of course, are known for their horrible odor, and as smelly pig farms go, the Pickton farm apparently smelled pretty darn bad. The family never could quite scrub the smell off themselves, and the kids were routinely ridiculed for the aroma that followed them around. Among the local brats, the Pickton children were universally known as the "Piggies". His siblings took this admittedly unimaginative moniker in stride and soon sloughed it off, but for Robert, the childhood taunt would continue to carry a sting for many years to come.

In 1955, at the age of six, Robert Pickton was enrolled in Millside, the local elementary school. Without any real training in manners or social interaction at home, the young Pickton was understandably awkward and shy around his classmates. His test scores suffered as a result, and he made bad grades in just about every subject. His second year in school wasn't much better than the first, and it was determined that he would have to be held back a grade so that he could catch up with his peers. When he finally did reach the third grade, he was placed in the closest thing 1950s Canada had to a class for special needs students. He would remain in special education classes for the rest of his time in the school system.

In 1963, when he was 13, Pickton matriculated at Mary Hill Secondary School, but he eventually dropped out due to the intense ridicule that he continued to face for his offensive odor and his inadequate intellect. The playground bullies were constantly picking on Pickton, and the pressure drove him away from school for good. And just as society had rejected Pickton, it wouldn't be long before Pickton would thoroughly reject society.

The Piggy Palace

After he dropped out of school, Robert Pickton's life consisted mainly of taking care of the farm and looking after his aging parents. Unlike his youthful peers, Willie wasn't known for drinking, carousing, or even dating. The only real pastime he had was writing to his pen pals. In the age of Facebook and Snapchat, the practice of writing a note on a piece of paper and physically mailing it to someone has come to seem downright archaic, but this is what Pickton enjoyed doing on a regular basis. The pen pals he wrote to were women that he would never have had the nerve to speak with in person. Much like a modern teenager who can chat up a storm in an instant messenger but fail to carry a conversation face-to-face, Pickton poured his heart out to his faceless pen pals.

He was particularly fond of a young woman named Connie Anderson who lived in Pontiac, Michigan. At the age of 24, in the year 1974, he actually made a trip out to see her. It was quite an adventure for the young Pickton. Traveling by bus, he passed through several cities along the way, and at some point, he was even accosted by a modeling agency. As he remarked years later in recollection to a friend, "I'm a plain old farm boy. They want me for a model? A model? Me? Forget it."

According to Pickton, by the time he left Connie Anderson's residence, he and Connie were engaged. However, while Pickton considered his erstwhile pen pal the "love of his life", she couldn't leave her job and he couldn't leave the farm. Their romance fell through the cracks, and not long afterward Leonard and Louise died from prolonged illness.

When both of his parents passed away in the late 1970s, Pickton inherited a considerable amount of property. But although his brother Dave and his sister Linda received full rights immediately, Robert's portion would be sealed away in a trust until he reached the age of forty. Pickton bitterly debated his siblings on this measure for several years afterward, but in the end, all he could do was bide his time.

During the 1980s he lived a quiet life on the farm, focusing mostly on his passion for acquiring new vehicles. His pride and joy was the 1977 Ford truck he had purchased with $20,000 of cash inherited from his mother. He also liked to visit the local automobile auctions, where he would buy and sell car parts.

Pickton also managed to maintain his parents' former client base in the meat market. They would hire him to represent them at livestock auctions. He would be there just about every Saturday, buying rabbits, geese, goats, and even lamas. Every weekend, whatever it was his customers asked him to get, he would get it. When he brought the animals back to the farm he would butcher them, usually after slitting their throats with a knife. Larger animals he would shoot in the head with a nail gun.

One can only imagine how strange and lonesome his life was, dwelling in solitude on a big, desolate, and disgusting farm, his only regular company the animals he slaughtered. But things would soon change. His older brother Dave, who had started a successful construction business, and his sister Linda, who had found a niche for herself in real estate, concocted a plan to make some money off of the large tracts of unused land on the property.

By the early 1990s several portions of the land had been sold off and repurposed, and in 1994 developers called Eternal Holdings purchased several acres on the east side of the farm to build a series of townhouses. The company gave the Picktons a whopping 1.76-million-dollar payout. With this one deal, the siblings, who had grown up threadbare and poor, became multi-millionaires.

In 1996, Robert Pickton's ever-inventive brother and sister registered part of the farm as a nonprofit charity which they gave the decidedly odd moniker of "The Piggy Palace Good Times Society". They claimed that their new "charity" would "organize, coordinate, manage and operate special events, functions, dances, shows, and exhibitions on behalf of service organizations, sports organizations, and other worthy groups." This unusual-sounding "charitable organization", however, soon developed a reputation not for good works but for hosting drunken revelries with thousands of people in attendance.

The unsavory attendees at these gatherings included Hell's Angel bikers and a steady stream of prostitutes from nearby Vancouver; the parties became famous for outrageous antics and over-the-top indulgence in alcohol and drugs; and had any of the guests been sober enough to think about it, they would have realized that such chaos would end up on police radar sooner rather than later.

It was actually Dave whose activities on the farm first fell afoul of the authorities. After several stolen cars were located on the property, he was accused of running a chop shop for the Hell's Angels. When local residents heard of this unfolding investigation, most were not too surprised. Willie's bad-tempered brother had been having brushes with the law his whole life, and with the continual raucous partying on the farm, another such confrontation had seemed almost inevitable.

For Dave, such things were expected. Yet no one ever dreamed that his mild and seemingly simple-minded brother Willie could be guilty of any crimes. The odd but docile man seemed incapable of aggression, letting alone committing serial murder. But his placid facade was an easy cover for the more nefarious inner workings of his mind, and on March 23, 1997, his evildoing finally came to light.

Drugs, Guns, and Attempted Murder

For many Canadians, the year 1997 was a particularly bad one. Residents of Manitoba were devastated by the Red River Flood in April, with 40,000 fleeing the deluge which destroyed over 1,500 homes. But the citizens of Vancouver were facing a deluge of a different kind: a deluge of missing women in and around the metropolitan area.

It was a blatant crime, and yet little was known about the perpetrator. All anyone in Vancouver knew was that—like some monster out of a horror movie—some figure was lurking in the back alleys of Vancouver late at night to snatch his prey. By the light of day, the attacker was nowhere to be seen. Investigators were initially completely baffled as to who he might be. Little did they know that there was a true house of horrors—a slaughterhouse of horrors, to be exact—suppurating just outside of Vancouver city limits.

Because it was at the Pickton pig farm that many of these missing women met their grisly fate. These unfortunate souls were literally being chopped up into meat by a butcher named Robert Pickton. This was why police were not finding any bodies—they were being ground up like hamburger meat on Pickton's farm. Robert Pickton's slaughterhouse had become a point of no return, with none of his victims ever leaving the premises intact—or alive.

But that changed on March 23, 1997, when Pickton picked the wrong target and attempted to subdue a prostitute named Wendy Lynn Eistetter. Wendy was simply doing what she always did when she was desperate for money: turning a trick and selling herself for just 100 dollars. But she turned out to be worth much more than that to the innocent women of Vancouver because she proved to be much more formidable than anyone the deranged Pickton had ever dealt with before.

Pickton drove Wendy from Vancouver to his farm with every intention of brutalizing, maiming and murdering her like he had done to so many others, but he was in for a surprise that night. He always kept a pair of fur-covered handcuffs under the mattress where he took the women to do the deed. As was his custom, he positioned himself behind Wendy while she was in a state of undress, grabbed the handcuffs, and quickly slapped a cuff across one of her wrists.

Wendy, however, knew exactly what he was up to, and as soon as she felt the first cuff snap shut on her wrist, she was determined not to let him apply the other one. Running on pure adrenaline, she spun around, grabbed a knife Pickton had nearby, and lashed out, managing to stab him in the neck and arm. Stunned and injured, Pickton fell back, which allowed Wendy to get away from him and run full speed away from that house of horrors.

She made it off the pig farm and out onto the open road where—knife in hand, handcuffs still on her wrist—she flagged down a passing motorist who took her to the nearby Eagle Ridge Hospital. Here, while her injuries were being tended to, she reported the incident to the authorities. In a stroke of supreme irony, a short time later Robert Pickton arrived at the very same hospital to be treated for his stab wounds.

If the wounded Pickton didn't already look suspicious enough, the fact that medical staff found a set of keys in his pocket that perfectly fit the pair of handcuffs that had been snapped on Wendy's wrist certainly didn't help matters. Police took custody of Pickton's clothing as evidence, and since Pickton washed his clothes about as rarely as he washed himself, the soiled fabric would tell quite a tale—eventually.

Pickton's clothes contained not only Wendy's DNA but also that of two other missing prostitutes. However, this discovery was only made after the seized clothing sat inside an evidence locker for about seven years without any further follow-up. This was only the beginning of police bungling in the case, and after a very short stay in jail, Robert Pickton was released after posting a $2,000 bail.

Pickton was subsequently charged with a whole host of offenses ranging from unlawful confinement all the way to attempted murder. These charges never made it to trial, however; all were ultimately dropped by December of 1998. The Vancouver court system, which was often accused of being biased against "undesirables" such as the city's sex workers, apparently had little interest in pursuing the case.

But even though Pickton had escaped the long arm of the law, for the time being, he could not escape the local zoning board. His property was cited for violating zoning regulations on the grounds that it was not actually being used as a farmstead. The Picktons, however, simply chose to ignore the board's ruling. They even held a raucous New Year's Eve party to ring in 1999—yes, just like the Prince song that was so popular at the time, the Picktons did indeed "party like it was 1999"!

Tired of fooling around, the authorities then slapped the Pickton property with an injunction authorizing police "to arrest and remove any person" taking part in such festivities. The property's nonprofit designation was rescinded a short time later, supposedly on the grounds of an "inability to procure financial statements". But even with these meager legal measures in place, women who came to Pickton's pig farm continued to disappear mysteriously.

In fact, that very same year, an informant came forward to report some hearsay that once again linked the missing women to Pickton's property. The informant claimed that a regular on the property, a troubled drug user named Lynn Ellingsen, had told him that she had seen the body of a nude woman hanging from a meat hook attached to the ceiling of Robert Pickton's slaughterhouse. However, when police questioned Ellingsen, she denied ever witnessing anything of the sort.

Several years later she would change her story and confirm that she had indeed seen a dead woman hanging from a meat hook. She claimed that she had stayed silent because Pickton was her number-one drug connection. Charming, right? She knew he was committing the worst of crimes, yet she opted to remain quiet about the whole thing so she wouldn't lose access to her drug supply!

It wasn't until early February 2002, that police finally got a search warrant for the premises, and once again their investigation had nothing to do with the missing women. This time they suspected that the Picktons were stockpiling illegal guns; a former farmhand had tipped them off to a large cache of weapons he had seen stashed on the property. The RCMP launched a surprise raid of the farm on February 5, 2002. It's not clear exactly how many illegal firearms were found, but there were enough that the Picktons were evicted and the police were given free rein to investigate.

After that, it wasn't long before authorities initiated a second investigation focusing on the missing women. This team discovered the first of what would be many personal items belonging to several of the women who had disappeared from

Vancouver. The next day, Pickton was indicted on weapons violation charges and brought into custody. He was again able to secure his release on bail, but this time he remained under tight police surveillance—and this time his freedom didn't last long. On February 22nd, Pickton was behind bars once again, charged with two counts of murder in the first degree.

Pickton Stands Trial

As he sat in jail with police combing through every inch of his property, Robert Pickton must have known that the jig was up. He must have considered the consequences and at least to some extent resigned himself to his fate. He knew exactly what the police would find on the farm, and he, no doubt, realized that there wasn't much point in even attempting to hide his guilt.

That's probably why he so readily related the full scope of his crimes to an undercover police officer during his stay at a jail in Surrey, British Columbia. Posing as just another inmate, this undercover cop struck up what seemed to be a friendly conversation with his new cellmate, but he had an ulterior motive. He was looking for a full confession from Pickton, and he received one. Pickton openly told the officer that he had been responsible for the deaths of 49 women. He also expressed some remorse upon revealing this fact—but not overkilling the women. Instead, he was sorry that he had been stopped just shy of 50! Apparently, it had been Robert Pickton's warped and deranged goal to kill a solid 50 people, and he was upset that the police had managed to stop him at 49!

But even without this stunning jailhouse confession, all of the grisly evidence Pickton left behind on his farm spoke for itself. The Pickton pig farm immediately became one of the largest crime scenes in Canadian history, only to be rivaled in recent years by the widespread killing grounds attributed to Bruce MacArthur.

With Pickton behind bars and a meticulous investigation of his property underway, the charges against him only multiplied. By early April, he had been charged with four more counts of murder in the deaths of Jacqueline McDonnell, Diane Rock,

Heather Bottomley, and Andrea Joesbury. Then, even while he awaited trial for those slayings, four more bodies were found and four more murder charges were leveled against him. October brought yet another four bodies, and four subsequent charges were made against him as well. It seemed that every month brought more bodies and more charges, and by the time court proceedings finally began on January 30, 2006, Pickton was standing trial on 27 separate charges of murder.

The case seemed like a slam dunk for the prosecution, but some people found it impossible to imagine that Robert Pickton had really committed such heinous crimes—including, possibly, some people on the jury. During the trial, one female juror allegedly remarked, "Pickton is innocent. There is no way he could have done this." When questioned, however, she denied making the statement, and since there was no proof she was allowed to remain on the jury.

To the surprise of many, when the verdict was reached on December 9, 2007, Pickton was found not guilty on six counts of first-degree murder. But although he was exonerated of the heftiest of the charges, there were more than enough murder charges to go around. Pickton was found guilty of six separate counts of second-degree murder, which automatically carries a life sentence in Canada.

Many in Vancouver no doubt hoped that this would be the last they would hear of the pig farm killer, but they were to be disappointed. In 2015, a film about the case tentatively titled *Full Flood* began production. It was ultimately released in 2016 under the title (borrowed from the Stevie Cameron book of the same name) *On the Farm*.

Even more jarring for the victims' families, however, was the news that Pickton himself had penned an account of his life from his prison cell and had passed it to a fellow inmate. This inmate took the manuscript with him upon his release, and in turn, passed it on to a retired construction worker and writer by the name of Michael Childress. And once the industrious Michael Childress got a hold of the material, it wasn't long before a full-fledged book was on the market.

Taking advantage of today's unparalleled self-publishing opportunities, Childress promptly edited and polished up this manuscript, slapped the title *Pickton: In His Own Words* onto the title page, and began to sell it on Amazon! Amazon has been pressured to remove the book, but only time will tell if the incarcerated Pickton and his collaborating cronies will make any further attempts to promote this alternative narrative of events.

Russell Williams
Trouble in Trenton

Flying High

Convicted Canadian serial killer Colonel Russell Williams actually wasn't from Canada; he was born to British parents, Cedric David Williams and Christine Nonie Williams, in Bromsgrove, England. But he was still a child when the family moved to Canada so that Cedric could take a job as a metallurgist at Chalk River Laboratories, one of the country's foremost nuclear research labs.

By all accounts, the early years in North America were happy and profitable for the Williams family. They were well liked and quickly made many new friends, including a Canadian couple named Jerry and Marilynn Sovkas. The Sovkas and Williams families soon became inseparable—a little *too* inseparable, as it turned out. Cedric was caught having an affair with Mrs. Sovkas, and Christine promptly filed for divorce. Shortly after the separation, Christine began to see none other than Jerry Sovkas. Mr. Sovkas then divorced Marilyn and married Christine, who took his last name and began to go by her middle name, thus becoming Nonie Sovkas.

It remains unclear whether the two couples were engaged in swinging or wife-swapping before the mutual dissolution of their marriages, but the suspicion is hard to avoid. At any rate, they certainly had an unusual degree of familiarity with each other. Needless to say, these soap-opera-style dramatics must have been very confusing and hard for six-year-old Russell Williams to process. He had no choice in the matter, however, and a year into his mother's new marriage, he too shed his old name in favor of a new one: Russ Sovkas. He would carry his stepfather's name until he decided to discard it as a young adult and revert to being Russell Williams once again.

During his school years, though, he was strictly known as Russ Sovkas. Russ and his newly blended family eventually moved to Scarborough Bluffs, Ontario, an affluent suburb of Toronto. Here he attended Birchmount Collegiate High School, where he was known as a fairly sociable and active young man. He had a part-time job delivering the paper and could be found playing the piano or trumpet in his spare time.

Another big change occurred in Russell's life when his stepfather took a job at a nuclear plant in South Korea. Leaving the comfy confines of suburban Canada for the Korean Peninsula would be quite an adjustment for anyone, but for the most part, Russell took it in stride. He returned to Toronto a year later, apparently none the worse for wear.

Russell completed his high school career at a prestigious private school called Upper Canada College, then enrolled at the University of Toronto at Scarborough, where he studied politics and economics. He also resumed using his birth name, introducing himself to classmates as Russell Williams.

Williams is said to have done well at the University of Toronto, both academically and socially, although his roommates noted his penchant for immature pranks. Many years later they could still recall the lengths to which he would go to trick, surprise or frighten them. Most disturbing in light of what the future had in store, he would sometimes pick the locks to his friends' rooms so that he could hide inside and wait for them to come home. He apparently got a real kick out of startling his unsuspecting classmates by jumping out at them and shouting "Surprise!" Despite his pranks and practical jokes, however, Williams was a serious and determined student who received his bachelor's on schedule in 1986.

He had also managed to take some flying lessons at the municipal airport, a skill that would serve him well in the coming years. Those who knew him at the time remember that he was practically obsessed with flying. When the Tom Cruise classic *Top Gun* came out, Williams could be seen in the movie theatres religiously watching the film over and over. His friend Jeff Farquhar was deeply concerned about the ritual, worrying that Williams was trapped in some kind of fantasy world.

If Williams was indeed fantasizing about being a military pilot, the dream became real less than a year later. Russell Williams joined the Canadian Armed Forces ("Canadian Forces" for short) in 1987 and graduated from flight school in 1990. Just like the Tom Cruise character in *Top Gun*, Williams had gotten his wings. He had proved to the world that he could fly high—but no one ever dreamed he would sink so low.

Rising through the Ranks

Russell Williams was on a quest to be the best, and it wasn't long before he started rising through the ranks. After an initial posting as a flight instructor at Canadian Forces Base Portage la Prairie in Manitoba, he was promoted to Captain in January of 1991 and transferred to the 434 Combat Support Squadron at CFB Shearwater in Nova Scotia. It was also around this time that he married a woman named Mary Elizabeth Harriman.

The young couple was on the move again in 1994 when Williams was reassigned to the 412 Transport Squadron in Ottawa. This post proved to be rather interesting for Williams as he was given the responsibility of guarding and transporting important officials, politicians, and ambassadors. He remained in this role until his promotion to Major in November of 1999. He received a master's in Defense Studies from the Royal Military College in 2004 and was then promoted to Lieutenant-Colonel. Later that summer he was given command of the 437 Transport Squadron at CFB Trenton in Ontario. By December of 2005, he was also serving jointly as commander of Camp Mirage, a covert logistics facility located in the United Arab Emirates.

These were not minor accomplishments. Williams was obviously well regarded in military circles for him to have been entrusted with two simultaneous commands which required him to fly back and forth across the globe. His career continued to advance when he was named the director of the Canadian National Defense Headquarters (NDHQ) in 2006.

His health, however, took a turn for the worse at this point. Williams developed a mysterious, lingering, chronic pain throughout his body. Such symptoms are not uncommon for veterans returning from the Middle East, but the cause remains unclear. Not knowing what else to do, Williams's doctor simply followed standard procedure and prescribed a cocktail of heavy pain medication, prednisone, and other drugs.

The drugs did ease his pain, but they had the side effect of frequent insomnia—and it was on some of these sleepless nights that Williams began to break into the houses of unsuspecting women.

Recent developments in his own domestic life facilitated these depraved escapades. Mary had recently been named as an associate director for the Heart and Stroke Foundation of Canada, and her new responsibilities forced her to spend most weeknights away from home. These wakeful, lonesome nights without his wife apparently provided Russell Williams with both motive and opportunity to act on some of his more insidious compulsions.

As far as investigators can tell, Williams began breaking into houses sometime in 2007. Initially, he would stake out a residence and wait until he was certain no one was home before making his entry. He would then rifle through dresser drawers looking for women's underwear and other intimate apparel. At first, these were just quick snatch-and-grab break-ins, but as he grew more confident in his craft, Williams began to linger longer. According to later testimony, on one of these panty raids, he stayed for nearly three hours trying on a young girl's pink undergarments, alternately posing for pictures and masturbating in her bed.

Williams carried out these intrusions with such precision most of his early victims had no idea that anyone had even been inside their homes. He did not force his way in; instead, he applied the locksmithing skills he'd picked up as a practical joker at the University of Toronto and simply walked through the front door. It is alarming to realize that your home and lingerie could be so violated without your knowledge—enough to make you think twice the next time you can't seem to find a pair of underwear! But much worse was in store.

Soon, Williams's compulsions mushroomed, and simply stealing undies from unaware victims was no longer enough. Soon, he began to reach out and inflict his perverted passions upon the owners of the undergarments.

The Split Personality

In the summer of 2009, Russell Williams began a steady escalation of the scope, boldness, and depravity of his crimes. At some point in July, he managed to hide inside a home while the owner was present. He waited and then watched from his vantage point while she took off her clothing before showering.

While it may seem hard to believe that Williams could do this completely unnoticed, you have to remember that this was a man who had recently been working at a secret overseas base. He had apparently become an expert at stealth. Although it's probably safe to say that the Canadian government never imagined that one of its soldiers would put his hard-won training to such nefarious use, Williams obviously had talent when it came to planning and executing clandestine missions. It's a shame that he didn't direct these skills toward more valiant goals, such as covert military rescue operations or the apprehension of enemy combatants. The same skillset he employed to sneak into the homes of innocent women could easily have been used to infiltrate the compounds of terrorist leaders instead.

But for whatever reason, Russell Williams took a decidedly different tack. And unfortunately for his targets, he was now ready to take things even further—he was preparing for his first sexual assault.

The incident occurred sometime in September of 2009. The woman he targeted was home alone with her infant daughter. She had fallen asleep when she woke to the sound of Russell Williams entering her home. Williams immediately overpowered her, binding and blindfolding her. With his prey completely helpless, Williams began fondling the bound woman's breasts.

After ordering her to take off her clothes, he took several photos of his frightened captive. Disturbingly enough, just a few hours after Williams engaged in this despicable activity, the insomniac soldier put on his good-guy face and made his way to a charity event being held by the Criminal Intelligence Service of Ontario.

Just a couple of weeks later, Williams's lustful compulsions got the better of him once again and he broke into the home of Laurie Massicotte. He had already conducted a couple of trial runs at Laurie's home on previous occasions, sneaking in when she wasn't home to steal her underwear and other items. Laurie was one of the many targets who never even suspected that they had been victimized, and when she was forced to confront the madman face to face she was taken completely unaware. She woke up to Williams striking her about the head, and she was soon blindfolded and bound.

Once his captive was secured, Williams began to play a long-drawn-out psychological game wherein he pretended to be a member of a group of burglars, assigned to the task of watching over her during the theft. At first, playing the strange role of a compassionate crook, Williams assured Laurie that she wouldn't get hurt as long as she didn't do anything to disturb the "others" as they rummaged through her home for valuables. Of course, these "others" that Williams referred to were just figments of his own twisted imagination.

Laurie was completely compliant, carefully following her captor's instructions, but Williams stuck to his own script. He was soon fondling her breasts, having her take off her clothes, and taking pictures. At one point she meekly requested, "Please don't put these on the internet", but beyond such sad protestations, she offered no resistance.

Laurie was heeding the advice of many criminologists, who suggest that the best thing to do when confronted with an armed assailant is to listen to their demands. The theory is, "Do what they say and you won't get hurt." Sadly, it doesn't always work out that way, and many completely compliant victims have been murdered despite their meek and mild manner.

Williams's next victim was not one of these, though. Her name was Mari-France Comeau, she was a 37-year-old Corporal in the Canadian Forces, and she was ready to put up a fight. Mari-France actually got the drop on Williams when she found his hiding spot in her basement. Upon being discovered, Williams lunged at her and struck her viciously several times with his flashlight. Mari-France put up a valiant fight, but Williams eventually overpowered her. For the next couple of hours, he beat, raped, and taunted his victim with his tape recorder running. While the video would not be shown during his trial, the chilling footage was seen by prosecutors who relayed the shocking details to the court. Like some sadistic cat toying with a mouse it had caught, Williams eventually grew weary of the twisted game he was playing and suffocated Corporal Comeau.

Just a short time later, as if nothing out of the ordinary had occurred, Colonel Williams reported to duty at NDHQ. If any killer ever had a diabolically split Jekyll-and-Hyde personality wherein deranged desires sat side by side with an ability to function well in normal society, it was Russell Williams.

Putting the Monster to Rest

After taking some time off for the holidays, Russell Williams returned to his hobby of performing sadistic acts of cruelty on complete strangers in January of 2010. His next victim was a woman by the name of Jessica Lloyd. He broke into her Belleville home and blindfolded her with duct tape before restraining her hands with a piece of rope. As was now standard procedure for Williams, he then spent the next few hours sexually assaulting her as she pleaded with him not to hurt her.

Williams then changed his tactics a bit by taking his captive back with him to his own home. If only the police had managed to intervene and arrest the psychotic killer before he reached his residence! They would have saved a life because once Williams brought Jessica home, after another several hours of prolonged torture, he murdered her and stashed her body in his garage. A couple of days later he dumped it further afield.

Jessica Lloyd's family knew something was wrong by that point and had already reported her as missing. Ontario police began to investigate her disappearance. Their first clue was a set of distinctive-looking tire tracks etched into the snow outside her residence. The police took note of the unique prints and continued their investigation. A week later, Williams just happened to get pulled over, and the officer noticed the similarity between his tires and the tracks that had been observed at Jessica Lloyd's home.

The officer let him go that night, but Williams was secretly placed under police surveillance as a result of the encounter. Investigators were able to match not only the tire tracks but also several footprints to the Colonel. On the strength of this circumstantial evidence, they brought Williams in for questioning.

After several hours of interrogation, he finally broke down and offered a full confession to his crimes, describing in exact detail how he had perpetrated his break-ins, rapes, and murders.

He then brought police to his home and handed over the collection of photos and videos he had taken during his assaults. During this remarkably forthcoming production of incriminating evidence, one of the stunned police officers asked Williams point-blank why he did what he did. Williams was equally blunt in his response: "I don't know the answers, and I'm pretty sure the answers don't matter." Even Russell Williams's warped mind knew that the jig was up. No matter what he said, it would neither bring the dead back to life nor save him for what fate had in store.

Williams was arraigned and incarcerated the next day, February 8, 2010. Once he was safely behind bars, investigators began to look into several break-ins that had occurred near where he lived. As the investigation heated up, Williams attempted to short-circuit it by taking his own life, cramming a cardboard toilet paper roll down his windpipe in the hope that it would suffocate him. Death by toilet paper roll isn't exactly the most glorious way to go, but Williams was apparently anxious to make his exit by any means possible. It didn't work, though, and after this incident, he was placed on suicide watch and closely observed 24 hours a day in solitary confinement. This vigilance managed to keep Williams alive to stand trial on October 18, 2010, when he pled guilty as charged.

Too many observers, Russell Williams appeared to be genuinely remorseful for his crimes, even tearing up on occasion. He didn't seem to be the typical cold sociopath who was only upset to be punished, such as Robert Pickton. Instead, Williams seemed like he was honestly ashamed of his crimes. Yet for whatever reason, he had become so caught up in his sick compulsions that he couldn't control himself.

Williams also wrote out detailed personal apologies to both Jessica's mother and Marie-France's father. These missives expressed how deeply sorry he was for snuffing out the lives of their loved ones. Perhaps even more telling was the letter he wrote to his wife, telling her, "Dearest Mary-Elizabeth, I love you. I am so sorry for having hurt you like this."

His wife had stood by Williams throughout the whole ordeal, and now that the light of day had been shone onto her husband's depraved, dark passions, he was forever lost to her. Even if he hadn't been given a life sentence, there was no way she could ever look at the man she loved in the same way again. It was as if some sort of terrible monster from a horror film had been lurking within her husband and been driven to the surface, showing itself for what it really was.

This case has absolutely baffled the experts. Williams seems to have begun his breaking-and-entering spree out of nowhere. How unusual is it for a highly successful and otherwise responsible man to suddenly decide to break into homes to steal underwear? And the progression of his crimes was just as bizarre. He began his indiscretions by simply letting himself into empty homes to rifle through women's lingerie. This then evolved into voyeuristically watching his prey in intimate moments when they were unaware. Next, he began to confront his victims, forcing them to undress and pose for pictures. His crimes then grew to include sexual assault—and finally, murder.

Psychologists will be scratching their heads over this case for some years to come, but at least the residents of Ontario will be sleeping a little easier at night. There really are no phantoms hiding in Canadian closets, or monsters under the bed, now that the evil of Colonel Russell Williams has finally been put to rest.

Bruce McArthur Stalking Toronto's Village

Growing Up in Ontario

He was known as a mild-mannered man— a hard worker who was polite and who always followed the rules. But this man who seemed to value law and order had a life that was beset by turbulence and uncertainty. His marriage of 20 years ended in the late 1990s after he slowly and laboriously came out of the closet as a gay man. His lifestyle changed rapidly after this, not only through expression of his sexual preference but also in the matter of geography. He moved from the country confines of small-town Canada to the urban excitement of the country's biggest city, Toronto.

Here he gained a conflicted reputation as a charmer, a smooth talker, as well as a man with a short fuse, ready to fly into a full-blown rage at a moment's notice. Some of his acquaintances simply can't imagine McArthur being capable of the crimes he is now accused of. Yet others say that Bruce McArthur had "serial killer" written all over him.

To be clear, before anyone in the court of public opinion wrongfully attempts to seal this man's fate, as of this writing McArthur has not yet had his day in an actual court. He is simply accused, and he has not yet been found guilty of any crime.

Bruce McArthur, the accused killer recently making headlines in Toronto, was born on October 8, 1951, in Woodville, Ontario. Woodville is a decidedly small town of just 650 people nestled in the Kawartha Lakes region, a fertile valley of farms and fields about 70 miles north of Toronto. Until this year, sleepy little Woodville was primarily known for its train stations and cheese factory—not for suspected serial killers.

Bruce's parents, Malcolm and Islay McArthur, were respectable members of the community who ran a small family farm that sometimes doubled as a foster home for troubled youth. At any given time, the McArthur family was hosting as many as 10 foster children. Here in the bucolic bliss of small-town Ontario, Bruce attended a school that seemed more suited to 1800s frontier life than the stereotypically suburban 1950s.

Located on the outskirts of Woodville, the one-room schoolhouse where Bruce learned the basics of reading, writing, and arithmetic couldn't possibly have been more rural in its character. Today the old schoolhouse has been remodeled into a single-family home, but this was where Bruce McArthur was educated throughout his childhood and adolescence.

His former classmates there were shocked to hear the news of his arrest. They all said that they remembered nothing at all untoward about his behavior in school. Far from being a delinquent, the Bruce McArthur they knew was a prim and proper goody-two-shoes who never took part in the mischief of his peers. Several classmates recall him being a kind of teacher's pet and tattletale. On various occasions when pupils were acting up or plotting teenage pranks, it was McArthur who spilled the beans to the school authorities.

For those who grew up in Woodville and passed their childhood years with Bruce in that one-room schoolhouse, it simply defies imagination that he could be accused of hurting anyone—much less of being a serial killer! In these earliest of days, there does not seem to have been any inclination towards violence or animosity in Bruce's character. He followed the rules, but not in a malicious way, and he was known as a charmer with a gifted set of vocal cords who often participated in local singing contests.

Bruce eventually left Woodville's one-room schoolhouse behind to attend Fenelon Falls Secondary School. Fenelon Falls had both a four-year and a five-year curriculum. The four-year diploma focused primarily on technical and artistic vocations, and it was this pathway that Bruce chose for himself. Once again, his peers at Fenelon Falls had only fond memories of him, and former classmates were universally shocked and dismayed to hear the news of his arrest. Marion Clark Luchies's reaction said it all as she screamed, "No! Oh my goodness, I can't believe it!"

So McArthur got along well at Fenelon Falls, and it was here that he met his future wife, Janice Campbell. Both graduated with high marks in 1970, but the caption underneath Janice Campbell's yearbook photo does seem somewhat ironic in hindsight—she listed her number-one pet peeve as "someone who can't decide what they want". For the future wife of Bruce McArthur, a man who would one day end their marriage with an abrupt change in his sexual orientation, it was a foreshadowing of things to come.

When Janice Campbell became Mrs. McArthur, the young couple immediately moved to Toronto to make a new life for themselves. Neither one of them had solid employment or any prospect of a high-paying job in Canada's biggest city, but they took what they could and made the best of it. Their perseverance soon paid off, and McArthur landed a modest job at a downtown department store called Eaton's.

It is of interest to note that it was in the vicinity of this department store that Canada's "Gay Village"—a social hub for Canadian LGBT people— was first taking root at this time. The community was already beginning to flourish on Yonge Street, near the intersection of College and Wellesley, in the early 1970s. It is not clear, though, whether McArthur took any special interest in this up-and-coming area that was practically next door to his workplace, or if it was just a coincidence that he happened to work nearby.

More disturbingly, unexplained murders and disappearances began to occur in the neighborhood right around the time that McArthur arrived on the scene. To be clear, for all we know, this is just another coincidence, but many people are openly speculating about the potential for McArthur's involvement.

By all available accounts, though, Bruce and Janice maintained a quiet married life during this period. A coworker of McArthur's, a man named John Foot, has come forward with some insights on what McArthur was like at the time. Foot, a former vice-principal who was thoroughly shocked to hear of McArthur's arrest, describes him as a completely congenial, affable, and social man who never showed any aggression or anger and got along well with everyone he encountered. Foot also met Janice, and after observing the young married couple together he came away with the impression that theirs was a truly happy union.

The pair's only real difficulty occurred in 1978 when McArthur's mother passed away from a brain hemorrhage. He was devastated by the loss, and his sadness was compounded by his father's death just a few years later in 1981. Life went on, however, and the couple soon purchased their first house together and had two children, Todd and Melanie. Friends, coworkers, and neighbors say that the family always displayed the spitting image of normalcy during their tenure at the large brick house in suburban Oshawa, right on the shore of Lake Ontario.

Along with an idyllic new residence, McArthur had also picked up new employment as a traveling salesman for McGregor Socks. This job had McArthur leaving for long periods to travel from town to town—and while most young husbands and fathers would not enjoy being away from home so much, McArthur seemed to relish it. It is this key point that has led some to insinuate that perhaps McArthur engaged in homicidal activity along his sales route, meaning that his list of victims would be much higher than currently alleged. But before we start pointing fingers, connecting dots and jumping on the serial killer bandwagon, let's step back, take a deep breath, and consider the facts. McArthur has not been convicted of murder as of this writing, and this is all just speculation.

Unproven allegations of wrongdoing aside, what we know for a fact about McArthur's life as a traveling salesman is that he was very good at his job. He became quite successful and was soon selling his wares throughout most of Ontario. He was doing so well at one point that he even hired on extra help as "counters" for his ever-growing stock of socks and underwear. This team of underlings was given the task of tracking, preparing and ordering merchandise for the burgeoning business.

John Foot remembers McArthur as being completely meek and mild, a "kind of Caspar Milquetoast guy" (referring to an old comic strip character of like mentality), but this mild-mannered salesman was also a real go-getter. McArthur's business instincts and the connections he developed led him to partner with well-known retailers such as Sears and Hudson's Bay.

Unfortunately for the McArthur family, the fat years didn't last, and in 1993 McArthur's sock and underwear empire collapsed completely. McArthur was now struggling to earn a living, and prospects for the future suddenly seemed uncertain. And in the midst of this financial uncertainty, his son Todd somehow picked up the disconcerting habit of pranking random people with vulgar phone calls.

At first, the family chalked these acts up to the immature behavior of a bored adolescent. But the phone calls proved to be a much greater compulsion than anyone had realized. No matter how many times he was warned to stop, Todd just kept right on calling. It seemed that he had a real addiction. As a result, he soon ran out of warnings and faced stiff legal retribution in the form of fines and restraining orders. The fines pushed the family finances into free-fall, and the McArthurs were forced to mortgage their home in 1997.

Bruce and Janice's marriage was under obvious strain, but they still managed to get at least one vacation in. Caretaker Glen Macleod recalls encountering the couple in July of 1997 when they vacationed on Prince Edward Island. The excursion had been put in gear by a relative of Macleod's who went to church with the couple. The woman apparently felt sorry about the couple's recent hard times, and she offered to let them stay free of charge in one of the summer homes that Macleod took care of.

The McArthurs took the kind woman up on her generous offer and stayed in the home for two nights, taking in the local sights during the daytime hours. Although the trip ended up being a failure in terms of patching up their disintegrating marriage, McArthur made quite a good impression on Macleod, who recalls him as being a "fine gentleman" who seemed to be "soft-spoken and easygoing".

When Macleod saw on the news that the man he had become acquainted with on Prince Edward Island in the late 1990s was accused of several murders, he was shocked—and not only at the charges. He was also surprised by McArthur's general appearance. The McArthur he'd known was a neat, very slim, and meticulously dressed man. Macleod barely recognized the overweight, stocky, rough-and-tumble landscaper who began to haunt the pages of tabloid newspapers.

At any rate, the McArthurs' 1997 sojourn at Prince Edward Island was followed by bankruptcy in 1999. It was against this backdrop that the family man Bruce McArthur slowly began to open the door of the secretive closet he had long locked himself into.

Life in the Village

Surely his wife must have had some inkling that this was coming? According to former friends and acquaintances, McArthur's homosexual tendencies were almost an open secret. Just about everybody he met came away with the suspicion that he might not be completely heterosexual. While everyone was surprised to hear of his arrest, his coming out of the closet seemed completely predictable to most of the folks he had crossed paths with.

Once McArthur did declare his intention to live a completely homosexual life, it didn't take long for him to leave his wife. Janice seems to have accepted his decision and taken it in stride, even remaining friends with him after the dissolution of their marriage. It was Todd—who was 17 at the time of the divorce—who took the news the worst. Todd couldn't seem to accept his father's desire to live out his life as a gay man, and his own negative behavior and brushes with the law increased, apparently as a direct consequence of the rage he felt. Todd, it seems, felt abandoned when his father decided to choose a free-spirited homosexual lifestyle over his family.

Records indicate that the McArthur family home was sold in 2000. Bruce moved to an apartment in Toronto, near the same Gay Village that had been growing around the department store where he worked in the 1970s. He soon entered into an on-again, off-again relationship with a man named Skandaraj Navaratnam. Lovingly remembered by his friends and family simply as "Skanda", Skandaraj would go missing in 2010, becoming one of McArthur's alleged victims.

Sadly, Skanda's remains would finally be found in February of 2018 buried in a planter box on a property connected to McArthur's landscaping business. It was a horrible day for

Skanda's brother when he had to break the news to their 80-year-old mother, who had been carefully kept in the dark about her other's son's whereabouts. Family members were concerned that the elderly Ms. Navaratnam, who is a heart patient, wouldn't be able to handle it. They had tried to shield her from the unfolding tragedy, but when Skanda's death was confirmed, they could no longer prevent her heart from breaking.

In the early 2000s, though, Skanda was still alive and well, and McArthur was settling into his new lifestyle in the Village. He soon became a regular, if low-profile, fixture on the bar-and-festival scene.

Then, in 2001, less than a month after he turned 50, he was arrested for severely beating a significantly younger man with a metal pipe. The two met each other on the night of October 31st, Halloween, and the young man apparently took McArthur up to his apartment to "show him his Halloween costume". But somewhere in the midst of this holiday revelry, things took a grim turn. McArthur, opting for a devious trick rather than a treat, snuck up behind the youth and repeatedly struck him on the back, shoulders, and back of the head with the metal implement he had been literally hiding up his sleeve. The young man initially lost consciousness under the savage beating, but he was eventually able to wake up and call the police, whereupon he was taken to St. Michael's hospital and treated for his injuries.

McArthur cooperated with authorities, claiming that he had blacked out and didn't know why he'd done it. He entered a plea of guilty to assault with a deadly weapon but was not sentenced until April 11, 2003, when he received less than two years for the crime. At the sentencing, McArthur put on an apologetic face and stated, "I just want to apologize to the court for what happened. My life's been kind of a mess in the last year and a half, knowing what's going to happen and what's happened to me." The man to whom McArthur was apologizing was (now retired) Ontario Court Justice William Bassel. McArthur must have found a sympathetic ear in Justice Bassel because compared to other cases of such clearly premeditated and potentially deadly assault, the sentence was exceedingly light.

In at least this one instance, McArthur was caught red-handed engaged in a violent assault. Although he claimed to have blacked out, the fact that he walked up to an apartment with a metal pipe concealed on his person did not tend to back up that claim. With no hope of any other defense, all McArthur could do was throw himself on the mercy of the court—and in this case, it worked.

Also factoring into the leniency of the sentence was the fact that his victim wished to remain anonymous and did not fully cooperate with the investigation. Sadly, this is often the case with crime in the LGBT community, since many who have not revealed their lifestyle to their families wish to keep their identities secret. This was apparently the situation of McArthur's victim and the reason that he refused to give a victim impact statement.

Another factor that aided the defense was that McArthur's attorneys were able to argue that an anti-seizure medication he had been taking (known as "poppers" in the gay community, where it is used recreationally) could have caused him to black out and become violent. While this glossed right over the fact that McArthur arrived at the apartment already armed with the pipe, this meant that they could essentially blame the drug and not the person.

In the end, McArthur did not have to spend one day in prison. Instead, he served a year of house arrest. After this year was up, based on his good behavior and adherence to the rules, he was given a six-month curfew that allowed him out until 10 PM. This was followed by three years of probation. Beforehand, he underwent a psychiatric evaluation which produced a personality assessment that in retrospect seems decidedly flawed. It offered mainly positive feedback and even the hopeful prognosis that "there is a low risk that Mr. McArthur will re-offend."

So on the strength of this glowing report, McArthur was allowed to slip back into society—although not back into his old stomping grounds in the Gay Village. As part of his probation, McArthur was ordered not to possess any drugs other than those prescribed by a licensed physician; to stay at least 10 meters (33 feet) away from the beating victim's home and workplace, and to stay away from the Gay Village.

No longer able to meet guys for hookups in person, McArthur soon turned to the internet in search of new companions—and it wouldn't be long before these ephemeral love interests would begin disappearing.

All the way back in 2002, while his assault case was still pending, McArthur registered an account with the gay fetish site Recon. He created a full profile, expressing his interest in bondage, masochism, and submissive men. It seems that even while McArthur was preparing his sentencing speech expressing his regret for beating a man with a pipe during one of his rough and rugged excursions, he was seeking new submissive men on whom to perpetrate further acts of sexualized aggression. Along with his profile on Recon, McArthur could soon be found on the homosexual dating websites Manjam, Grindr, Bear411, and Silverdaddies. He often went by a username that referred to himself as a "silver fox" or something similar.

Once his probation expired, McArthur wasted no time in returning to the Gay Village scene. One man who befriended him during this time period was a Village regular named Robert

James. Robert first met McArthur in 2007 and had already begun to hang out with him before others who remembered McArthur's checkered past advised him against it. When Robert then attempted to distance himself from McArthur, McArthur didn't take it too well.

He first attempted to pull Robert back into his orbit through gentle persuasion, but upon being rejected he exploded into an angry, epithet-laden tirade, allegedly screaming, "I'm so tired of these fucking faggots telling stories about me! Why do you hate me so much?" Of course, hearing McArthur voice his red-faced rage in this manner only convinced Robert to heed the advice of those same "storytellers" and get the hell away from Bruce McArthur.

Realizing that he couldn't convince Robert to stay, McArthur screamed out the parting words, "You're just like the rest of them, you think I'm crazy!" It isn't clear exactly what, if anything, Robert said in response. But one can only imagine that after bearing the brunt of McArthur's verbal onslaught, Robert was quietly nodding to himself, "Yep, I think you're crazy, alright!"

Incredibly enough, despite the rumors and these continued bursts of anger, McArthur was able to secure a full pardon of his 2003 conviction in April of 2008! With his past transgression stricken from the official record, he now felt that he had the fresh start he needed to begin his life anew and restart his landscaping business. Thanks to this second chance, it wasn't long before he would resurface in the Gay Village, on landscaping projects, and even as a mall Santa Claus.

The Bad Santa

It boggles the mind how a man who had been convicted of beating another human being nearly to death with a metal pipe could be hired on to be a mall Santa. Since the role involves being around children, you would think that applicants would be subject to the most thorough of background checks—procedures that would even turn up a pardon such as McArthur received. It would then be up to the employer whether to honor the pardon or to determine the applicant to be ineligible for the position.

As it turns out, when McArthur worked at the Agincourt Mall in Toronto he was hired through a staffing agency. So the responsibility to sort through his background fell squarely on the shoulders of that agency. It's not clear what (if any) background checks they ran on him, but he appears to have sailed through them with flying colors. Thankfully, his time at the mall does not appear to have had any negative consequences. As the Agincourt Mall maintained in an official statement, "There were no reported incidents by customers or by store and mall employees during his [Bruce McArthur's] time at the mall".

Nevertheless, you can't help but feel a chill run down your spine when you see the TV news broadcasts and newspaper articles that show the same man accused of multiple murders grinning in full Santa Claus garb at the local mall. This was a sentiment that was well expressed shortly after MacArthur's initial murder arrest. Many found their way to McArthur's Facebook page, where pictures of him in the Santa getup were still in circulation, to express their horror and disbelief—and in some cases, dark humor. One poster left the telling comment, "This Santa made it to the naughty list". And another commentator simply left behind the hashtag "#killersanta". But although some have found some humor in a very serious situation, those directly affected by the crimes are certainly not laughing.

When Skandaraj Navaratnam disappeared in 2010, it was up to his distraught brother to find him, and in the end, the trail led to his brutalized remains buried in the bottom of planter boxes from McArthur's landscaping projects. But before the tragic end results of the investigation into Skanda's whereabouts came to light, McArthur would face his first rounds of police questioning—not as a suspect, but as a potential witness.

By 2012, other men from the Gay Village had begun to disappear, and Toronto police created task force called Project Houston to look into the matter. It was while they were investigating the disappearance of two gay men who frequented the Village—Abdulbasir Faizi and Majeed Kayhan—that they came to McArthur's door requesting an interview. McArthur had become associated with the men by means of dating apps which revealed ongoing communications he had with them shortly before they vanished.

Since the two men were both married and seeking to keep their homosexual affairs secret, they had covered their tracks well, and it had been incredibly hard for investigators to find reliable leads. They had learned of the connection to McArthur through a friend of Majeed's who had last seen him while he was with McArthur on a date set up through the app. Although the informant did not know McArthur's real name, he was well aware of his "Silverfox" username, and after he supplied it, police just had to do a simple search of the dating site to find McArthur.

McArthur then became a person of interest, but as the police would later put it, the case was difficult to prosecute "without bodies". As such police remained in what was essentially a surveillance role for the time being.

Making matters even more difficult, in late 2013 investigators got thrown a complete curveball when they received a false tip about a man named James Alex Brunton. As farfetched as it may sound, Brunton was accused of leading a ring of cannibals who were literally eating the missing men from the Village. But after an extensive investigation, police found no evidence of Brunton being involved in any disappearances or murders—let alone cannibalism.

They did discover that Brunton had been secretly recording teenage boys in a locker room, and he was prosecuted and convicted for voyeurism. But even with this successful side conviction, the fact that Brunton had turned out to be a dead end when it came to the missing gay men of the Village led those in charge to pull the plug on the official investigation into the disappearances. Project Houston was disbanded at the end of 2013, leaving the search for the missing men back at square one.

But even though the police had temporarily fallen off McArthur's trail, it wouldn't be long before he would put them right back on it. In 2016 McArthur is alleged to have met up with a man named Peter Sgromo at a local McDonalds. Although never a close friend, Peter had known McArthur in and out of his social circle in the Village for the better part of a decade. This familiarity probably helped to ease any lingering suspicions when the burly landscaper hit him up through the dating app Bear411 and arranged for a get-together.

The two at first spent the evening in casual conversation, just chit-chatting and catching up on old times together. As they were about to part, however, Peter walked with McArthur to his van and gave him a hug and a quick kiss to wish him goodbye. The two then began to kiss each other passionately, and McArthur offered to drive Peter back to the hotel that he was staying in.

Peter agreed, but when he climbed into the van, he saw something that gave him pause: The van was completely stripped down in the back. Still, no alarm bells rang; Peter rationalized what he saw by telling himself that McArthur probably hauled stuff for his job. It wasn't long before McArthur invited Peter into the back of the van with him, and the two began to engage in foreplay. McArthur was taking things a little bit too fast, however, and is said to have aggressively shoved the other man's head toward his crotch.

Peter protested and struggled free, but with a surprising show of tremendous strength McArthur grabbed him by the throat and shoved his head back down again. As Peter recalls, "Then he really grabbed my neck, violently twisted it, right to his crotch, and his pants were undone. That's when I really was quite disturbed." This time—as the victim claims—McArthur was choking him, literally squeezing the life out of him. Fortunately, Peter had taken some self-defense courses, and using a maneuver that one of his instructors had taught him, he was able to pinch a nerve in McArthur's elbow, forcing him to let go as he howled in pain. Peter then shouted, "Bruce, what are you doing?!?", and McArthur finally relented and took the rattled man back to his hotel.

But no matter how much McArthur tried to smooth things over, his would-be victim was still threatening to call the police when they parted company. Apparently getting very concerned at this point, McArthur tried to head his alleged victim off at the pass by driving directly to the 41 Division police station in Toronto to report his version of events. He told the duty officer there that "someone is going to report a sexual assault, but it's not true".

McArthur claimed that the act had been consensual and that Peter had merely changed his mind afterward and decided to fabricate a story of assault. Shortly after McArthur delivered this preemptive explanation, sure enough, Peter did indeed ring up the police station claiming that McArthur had assaulted him. In the end, it was just one man's word against another's, and since no one had been injured, the police didn't take the case too seriously. No charges were filed against McArthur.

The next known close call with McArthur occurred during an encounter with Gay Village regular Sean Cribbin in 2017. McArthur had met Sean the usual way, through various dating apps such as Recon and Growlr. On these apps, Sean saw a smiling, jolly man with pictures of himself dressed as Santa Claus. He thought the man might be a bit eccentric, but basically congenial and harmless. Even though he now considers the Santa pictures to be "creepy", back then he shrugged them off, thinking, "Oh, he does community work."

Following a series of intermittent exchanges, the two finally arranged a day to meet up in the summer of 2017. After arriving at their designated meeting place, Sean got into McArthur's vehicle to make the trip to McArthur's apartment. Sean recalls mostly just small talk during the ride, but when he mentioned rumors of a serial killer stalking the Gay Village, McArthur grew silent and quickly changed the subject. Instead of remarking on the rumors, he began talking about his landscaping business. In retrospect, Sean thinks that this is no coincidence since many of the remains of the alleged victims have emerged from various properties linked to McArthur's landscaping enterprise.

The only other thing that McArthur found pertinent to mention was that he had a roommate, but he was going to be at work and wouldn't interfere with their date. Nevertheless, Sean says that the two didn't waste any time once they arrived at McArthur's apartment. Sean, following McArthur's directions, went to the bathroom to put on the bondage gear that McArthur wished him to wear while McArthur went to the kitchen to mix him up a drink laced with the date rape drug GHB.

It is important to clarify that although GHB is indeed known as a date rape drug, it has long been popular in the gay community as a recreational drug to induce euphoria and heightened sexual feeling. Recreational use such as this involves only small doses so that the participant does not lose control of motor function. As Sean himself describes it, "GHB is a drug that causes euphoria. It puts you at ease and makes you comfortable. But there is a fine line with GHB." Knowing this to be the case, Sean specifically requested that McArthur mix only about 5 milliliters of the drug into his beverage so that he wouldn't become unduly incapacitated.

But soon after drinking the cocktail that McArthur had brewed, Sean knew that something was wrong. As the drug took hold of his body, he began to have heart palpitations and felt as if he couldn't breathe. Sean was fighting for control of his motor function when McArthur took advantage of the situation, knocking him to the ground before unbuckling his own pants and sticking his penis in Sean's mouth. This is not exactly dinner table conversation, but as Sean describes it, "He [McArthur] wasn't respecting my limits. He was basically raping my mouth with his penis."

It was a blatant violation, and things soon got worse when McArthur drove his penis down Sean's throat and managed to cut off his airway completely. Sean was already struggling to breathe, and now his oxygen was completely blocked off. At this point, he blacked out and went unconscious as McArthur continued his macabre sexual ritual with his comatose form.

But Sean came to less than a minute later to find his airway clear and McArthur hurriedly moving about the room. McArthur's roommate had apparently come home early, interrupting the assault and providing Sean with a much-needed reprieve. As he struggled to regain his composure, he told his attacker, "Oh, your roommate is home! I guess I'd better go." Sean claims that McArthur wasn't completely convinced and gruffly responded, "No—Not until I come first." But Sean, with McArthur's marauding member removed from his mouth, was now free to take in deep breaths of air and had regained his strength. He stood up and began to gather his things, insisting that he had to go. McArthur then reluctantly agreed.

Even though Sean was deeply disturbed by the encounter, he tried to put it behind him—until, that is, he received a phone call from the police shortly thereafter. It was then that he learned that Bruce "Bad Santa" McArthur had been very bad indeed. He had actually taken pictures of Sean while he was unconscious—in what the police described to him as nothing short of a "kill position".

The Evidence Begins to Pile Up

In the summer of 2017 a new task force, Project Prism, was created following the disappearance of two more men from the Gay Village—Selim Esen and Andrew Kinsman. It was Andrew Kinsman in particular who managed to galvanize the attention of the public and the police. Until this point, most of the victims had been relatively unknown, with many living double lives hidden away from their families. Kinsman, on the other hand, was not only out of the closet, he was a well-known gay rights activist in the community. He was also a volunteer at the local AIDS clinic and a bartender with a lot of friends.

As soon as Kinsman disappeared in June of 2017, everyone in his large social circle knew that something was desperately wrong. He vanished at the height of Canada's Pride Week—festivities that he was heavily involved in organizing for Toronto's LGBT community. His friends and family went into motion to find out what had happened to him almost immediately.

Leading the efforts were his two older sisters, Shelly and Patricia. They had often served as second mothers for their baby brother when they were all growing up, and they were devastated to hear the news. Even though Andrew Kinsman was a grown, 49-year-old man when he disappeared, his sisters would always remember him as a "young boy with long blond hair and bangs, wearing his tie-dye t-shirts and embroidered blue jeans, riding his mini-bike."

Just after Andrew vanished, his proactive sisters persuaded his landlord to let them into his apartment. Here they found his 17-year-old cat hungry, frightened, and all alone. Patricia and Shelly knew that Andrew, who doted on his long-lived cat, would never willingly have left it alone for so long. This keyed them off that something was definitely wrong, and they immediately expanded their search to the streets of the city and even nearby wilderness trails to see if they could find any sign of their little brother.

Sadly, it would be the investigators of Project Prism who would find what was left of Andrew Kinsman. His butchered remains were found at the bottom of a flower pot, just like those of so many other victims. The pot was on yet another property where McArthur had conducted his landscaping business.

Needless to say, McArthur had become the prime suspect in the case by this point, and he was now under round-the-clock surveillance. One of the things that police discovered during this monitoring was that McArthur had sold his old van for scrap at a place called Dom's Auto Shop in Eastern Ontario. Some bloggers have jokingly referred to this now infamous garage as "Dahmer's Auto Shop" in reference to the serial killer Jeffrey Dahmer, who is known for cannibalizing his dinner dates. But although police did not find signs of cannibalism in McArthur's old stripped-down van, they did find traces of blood.

Dominic Vetere, the shop's owner, remembers that police showed up on October 3, 2017. They told him that they were canvassing auto parts businesses in order to track down a Dodge Caravan that had been sold as scrap by a certain Mr. Bruce McArthur. When they discovered that Dominic had been the one who bought the van, they gave him the van's VIN (Vehicle Identification Number) and asked him to run a check on it. Dominic obligingly ran the VIN through the shop's database, located it, and led them through a junkyard full of disabled vehicles to McArthur's van. He recalls that the detectives were "really excited" to find the van still intact and not yet smashed into scrap. At that point, he did not know exactly why the police were so desperate to examine this van before it was pulverized and sent to the scrap heap—but the news report announcing McArthur's arrest in January of 2018 certainly clued him in.

Police had gathered more evidence a month before that when they cloned McArthur's computer on December 4, 2017. Operating under a Canadian legal instrument known as a general warrant, they entered McArthur's home when he wasn't around—probably with the cooperation of his landlord—and copied all the data on his laptop to an external hard drive. Among the files, they found photos that McArthur had taken of several alleged victims, including Sean Cribbin. Some of these photos are said to show the corpses of missing men, placed in various poses.

With this digital evidence added to the physical evidence of the blood found inside McArthur's van, the police now had everything they needed to move in. They just had to find the right time to do it, and that came on January 18, 2018, during an extended stakeout of McArthur's Thorncliffe Park apartment. While conducting their routine surveillance operations, officers observed McArthur bringing a young man up to his residence. Believing that the youth was at serious risk of injury or death, they decided to make the arrest. Using the warrant they had obtained after their discovery of blood in McArthur's junked van, police literally kicked in the door and stormed into his apartment.

The officers found McArthur's young visitor tied to a bed. Although he appeared to be under duress, he was physically unharmed. What else police discovered in McArthur's apartment has not yet been made public, but it seems that this is where they obtained the additional evidence they needed to charge him with homicide. Some sources suggest that this evidence came in the form of disturbing images of deceased victims that put McArthur directly at the crime scene. No human remains had yet been found, but officials stated at the time that even without a body, they "had a pretty good idea of how" McArthur's alleged victims had been murdered.

McArthur was initially charged with the murders of Skanda and Andrew Kinsman, and Police Detective Hank Idsigna began to give public briefings on the progress of the case. During one of these, he announced the possibility that a serial killer had been responsible for the Gay Village disappearances. Detective Idsigna also speculated that the suspect could be linked to multiple murders across Toronto spanning decades.

At this point, it is necessary to reiterate that McArthur has not been convicted of any murders yet. But Detective Idsigna and his team certainly have a sinking suspicion that a single killer has hidden uncounted victims in multiple burial grounds scattered all throughout the Toronto area. In February of 2018, Detective Idsigna revealed the suspected scope of the alleged crimes, calling the ongoing case "unprecedented" and stating that it might be connected to hundreds of unresolved missing person cases. In fact, as they combed through their cold case files, police realized they had an investigation that potentially went all the way back to 1975!

They obtained search warrants for five different locations where McArthur had done landscaping work. Four of these properties were within Toronto city limits, and the fifth was near the town of Madoc, Ontario. The Madoc property was owned by a fellow landscaper who had worked with McArthur in the past. The police were interested in all of these locations, but the big break came at a home in the Malory Crescent inside Toronto's Leaside residential community: It was at this residence that investigators found the first physical remains of some of the missing men.

McArthur was a regular at the property; he had a deal with the owners where he took care of the grounds in exchange for the privilege of storing his landscaping gear in their large garage. It was in this garage that the dismembered body parts of three different men were found buried at the bottom of planter boxes. McArthur was soon facing additional charges for murdering Majeed Kayhan, Soroush Mahmudi, and Dean Lisowick.

But this wasn't the end of the macabre treasure hunt at the Leaside home. In early February, Detective Idsigna made another grim announcement after the bones of another three men were unearthed from another set of planter boxes at the Leaside residence. Sadly for the family of Andrew Kinsman, some of these dismembered body parts belonged to him— although the only way to tell was from the prints on his severed fingers. With the identification of Kinsman, the case took on a whole new life as the friends and family of this pillar of the Gay Village community demanded a thorough and comprehensive investigation.

Once the alleged killer's modus operandi for concealing his crimes was discovered, many more planters were seized from various locations all over the Toronto area. Police deployed a wide array of equipment to unearth these remains, including ground-penetrating radar and even a tent with massive heaters aimed at the ground so the cold earth would be easier to dig up. Hundreds of cadaver dogs were also used to turn up a veritable mountain of evidence against the suspect.

All of this activity raised public curiosity to a fever pitch. In response, the police held an exhaustive Q&A session on March 5th, during which they displayed a picture of an unknown man's dead body. They explained that they believed that the man was McArthur's "seventh" victim and asked for help in identifying him. They knew that he had been homeless for many years and had long ago lost contact with his family, and as he had carried no photographic ID they deemed it necessary to publicize his picture in hopes that someone would know who he was. This public display of a picture of the corpse of a deceased citizen sparked considerable outrage among many, but despite the controversy, the photo was successful in generating more than 500 new tips.

The investigation progressed quickly, and by April 11th McArthur had been indicted on charges of murder for all the men in both the Houston and Prism investigations. He is currently being held in segregation and under suicide watch at the Toronto South Detention Centre, and so far his isolation has only been interrupted by a few court appearances—two in January and one in May.

For his debut in court, McArthur appeared on January 19th, accompanied by attorney Marianne Salih of Edward H. Royle & Partners Law Firm. Appearing downcast and subdued in grey slacks and a dark shirt, McArthur stood quietly while Salih made a motion to ban outside publication of trial proceedings. The motion was granted, putting a tight clamp on information coming out of the courtroom from that point forward.

However, it is known that McArthur was in court once again on January 29th, this time dressed in the standard orange jumpsuit of an inmate and represented by W. Calvin Rosemond. Rosemond is an experienced trial attorney known for his many successful homicide defenses. For his part, McArthur is said to have mostly just stared at the floor as he mumbled short, monotone answers to the judge.

The next legal proceeding was a pretrial hearing which was held on June 20, 2018. The trial itself is scheduled to start soon.

Continuing Controversies about the Case

From the very beginning, several controversies have swarmed around this case. It has been alleged that investigators were biased against both the gay community and the fact that most of the victims were immigrants. Some say that police were only galvanized to act by the disappearance of Andrew Kinsman, a man born and raised in Canada. Finding missing members of the immigrant community, it's alleged, was less of a priority.

Gay rights activist Nicki Ward claims that police should have known that a killer was on the loose in the Gay Village but blatantly ignored and dismissed the mounting evidence. As Ward put it, "Ignore, dismiss, diminish; these are all words that accurately describe the way police have dealt with missing persons in our neighborhood."

Authorities dispute this charge, however, maintaining that they carried out their investigation as best they could with the information they had. They claim that it was simply a coincidence that their investigation ramped up with the disappearance of Andrew Kinsman; it just so happened that they got a break in the case shortly after he went missing.

The Toronto Police Department has also pointed the finger of blame back in the other direction, alleging that its investigation was hampered by a marked lack of cooperation on the part of the gay community itself. As Chief of Police Mark Saunders has described the situation, "We knew that people were missing and we knew that we didn't have the right answers. But nobody was coming to us with anything."

This remark stoked further outrage in the Gay Village, where many perceived it to be flippant at best and outright victim-blaming at worst. Others, however, support Saunders in his assessment, arguing that many members of the gay community really are reluctant to become involved with the authorities due to lifestyles that often include illegal drugs and male prostitution. Perhaps it was out of fear of being charged with something themselves that so many in the Gay Village stayed silent when the police started asking questions.

Meanwhile, University of Toronto Ph.D. candidate Sasha Reid has claimed that she stumbled upon the Project Houston data in 2017 and was clearly able to identify the pattern of an active serial killer. She asserts that she informed police of this in July of 2017, nearly six months before they would announce their own serial killer theory. Even though police were apparently not yet taking the threat seriously, back in 2017 Reid was already warning her students to be on their guard during any excursions to the Gay Village in Toronto.

The animosity between the Toronto Police Department and the LGBT community remained at a fever pitch for much of 2017, so much so that organizers of the annual Gay Pride festival banned police from that year's festivities. This was disheartening for those members of the Department who earnestly wished for improved relations, as well as creating a heightened security risk for Pride participants.

Ironically enough, McArthur seems to have sided with the police during this divisive time! A February 2017 post on his Facebook page showed a Gay Pride flag with the word "Pride" crossed out and a caption that read, "The Toronto Police can stand with me. I won't be at Pride without them". Posted one year before his imminent arrest, was this a last-ditch attempt to win the police over to his side through a display of solidarity?

In any event, the controversy has only grown since McArthur was arrested, and as the trial goes forward, the year 2019 will surely see more of the same.

Paul Bernardo
The Scarborough Rapist

Birth of a Devil

When Paul Bernardo was born in Scarborough General Hospital in Toronto, he had a visibly dark patch extending along the left side of his head. It was diagnosed as a blood clot, and it took six weeks before Baby Paul recovered and went home to join his family—parents Kenneth and Marilyn Bernardo and two elder siblings, David and Debbie.

The Bernardos moved when Paul was a year old. Marilyn's diary sketches him as composed and reserved compared to his brother and sister. But not all that she inked depicted him in a good light. Along with being boorish and obstinate, he was also awfully harsh and the least affectionate of the children.

He also continued to suffer from physical ailments. He was allergic to cotton lint, orchard grass, poplar, and several other things. He suffered from a speech disorder which required surgery and therapy when he was still mumbling inarticulately at the age of three.

Paul attended Elizabeth Simcoe Junior Public School from kindergarten through sixth grade. Things went well for the first few years. He had a quick mind and got good grades. He was also courteous and respectful.

However, school turned into a difficult experience for him around the time he turned nine. He was frequently bullied by upperclassmen who made fun of his surname, cornering him during breaks and passing uncouth comments like "smelly barnyard, dirty barnyard" until he ended up in tears.

Still, young Paul didn't let the abuse drive him into isolation. He was keenly interested in sports like soccer and baseball. He earned a lifeguard certificate at the local YMCA and also joined the Boy Scouts.

But while all looked rosy on the outside, the inward scenario was anything but. If only the beasts amidst us looked like what they are!

Kenneth Bernardo did not seem all that interested in fatherhood. He resented having to put up with hyperactive children who made unreasonable demands all the time, and although he did not beat them he often bawled them out, subjecting Paul to an upbringing of constant yelling and screaming.

Even worse, he was a pervert who molested his own daughter and another young girl before he was finally arrested. He was also a peeping Tom who routinely peered into the rooms of women of all ages.

As a result, Marilyn fell into severe depression and distanced herself from her family—literally; she moved into the basement of their house. She also became spiteful, and during a massive argument, she once revealed that Paul was not actually Kenneth's son. His father, she said, was her former boyfriend.

Basically, Paul's mother was calling him an out-and-out bastard, and he responded in vulgar kind by calling her a slut and a whore. The incident also triggered a lifelong antipathy towards the opposite sex.

The strained relationship between his parents and their lack of attention to him meant that Paul grew up as an unloved and emotionally unstable child.

Paul Bernardo graduated from high school in 1982 and enrolled in the University of Toronto to study business. His mind, however, was filled not with a thirst for knowledge but with quixotic desires which often led him to sexually humiliate his girlfriends in public. And he did have girlfriends; Bernardo was enigmatic and captivating and he attracted women easily. His door-to-door sales job with Amway also taught him various ways to enthuse and intrigue the fair sex.

Bernardo and his friends went bar hopping almost every night. They persuaded many pleasant faces and innocent minds to believe their lies before having their wicked way with their bodies. Bernardo followed a predictable pattern with all the women he desired and dated. At first, he was courteous, affectionate, and attentive. When convinced that the girl was completely smitten by him, he gave his beastly inclinations free rein.

Bernardo's sexual fantasies were already perfectly dreadful by the time he started college, and his forceful attitude, atrocious temper and appetite for submissive sex only grew with time. His girlfriends, who were sick of being beaten up and then forced to submit to anal sex, started dumping him. He let them go but threatened to kill them if they opened their mouths. From 1984 through 1986 he had a string of affairs which all lasted less than a month because of his highly demanding and abusive personality. Occasionally he even dated more than one woman at a time, and the attraction of his strangely magnetic personality was so strong that even after they found out about each other, both would remain with him—for a few weeks, at least!

Following graduation, Bernardo was offered a job as a junior accountant at Price Waterhouse in Toronto.

In 1987 he raped two young women aged 19 and 21 at a bus stop. This was just the beginning of a reckless rape spree. Bernardo's modus operandi was consistent: He attacked women between 18 and 25 years of age, standing aside while they got off the bus and then grabbing them from behind before dragging them towards nearby isolated areas and forcing himself on them for anywhere from 30 minutes to two hours.

Karla Homolka - Partner in Crime
A Match Made in Hell

In October of 1987, Bernardo saw Karla Homolka dining with her girlfriend at a Howard Johnson's, and something inside him stirred. It was like a scene from a romance novel. Bernardo strode up to their table and flirted outrageously with Homolka, his cocky attitude and charming demeanor all in tune with his devious mind. As she listened to him ramble about his job at the accounting firm, Homolka responded very strongly. She wasn't your normal 17-year-old girl; her sexual fantasies were very similar to Bernardo's. Homolka invited him to join them at their table, and their instant mutual attraction and her overly responsive body language had them in bed within a couple of hours.

Homolka satisfied his sexual appetites in a way no other woman had. She didn't mind submitting to his desires, and she even encouraged his sadistic attitude. Bernardo was a man who made her live her life on the edge, and she didn't give up on him even when he began calling her fat and ugly. Bernardo was extremely pleased. It excited him that Homolka didn't mind being handcuffed, and it excited him even more when she gave him a list of perverted sex acts and let him choose which one he wanted her to perform.

Bernardo began spending a lot of time with Homolka, and she was soon blindly in love with him. She was so determined to keep him interested in her that one day when Bernardo told her that he was literally a rapist, she said she thought it was cool! Such unquestioning devotion revved Bernardo's interest in Homolka to new heights, and this only reinforced her infatuation with him. Now nothing and no one could come in the way of keeping Bernardo chained to her. She indulged every last one of his horrid sexual demands and even began allowing him to bring willing—and unwilling—young girls into their bedroom.

By March of 1988, Bernardo had committed eight rapes and had come to be known as the Scarborough Rapist. Detective Steve Irwin, who took a dedicated interest in rape cases, was the first to identify the activity of a serial rapist. Police managed to collect a decent amount of physical evidence, but even so, the investigation did not progress quickly, and by 1989 the number of rapes had jumped to over 10.

Finally, a victim of a 1990 assault who distinctly recalled the rapist's face was able to assist the police in creating a composite portrait. The police released the picture to the media and it was published in newspapers in Toronto and the surrounding area.

Following this publicity, Bernardo participated in a 35-minute interview with two police officers. He readily agreed to give samples for forensic testing, and in general, he behaved like such a well-educated and gracious youth that the detectives began doubting themselves and released him. Such is the charm of the devil!

Bernardo was mingling with Karla's family more and more. After two years of dating, they were engaged and were soon to be married, but Bernardo continued to test Karla's intentions and commitment—this time by demanding the virginity of her younger sister! Bernardo had been indulging in obscene fantasies about 15-year-old Tammy Homolka ever since he met her for the first time. Stating that he was greatly upset that he hadn't been the one to claim Karla's virginity, Bernardo asked for Tammy's instead.

At first Karla was aghast at this proposition, but in the end, she caved in. She had become so dependent on Bernardo that she couldn't imagine life without him. On December 23, 1990, Karla drugged her younger sister with fifteen sleeping pills. She then took Tammy to the basement of her house, and Bernardo raped her while Karla videotaped the gruesome act. Horrible as this was, the situation only spiraled downwards when Tammy vomited and died of suffocation due to the overdose of sleeping pills. Bernardo and Karla somehow managed to avoid blame for Tammy's death.

Shortly thereafter the Scarborough Rapist mysteriously ceased his attacks. The reason was simple enough: Bernardo had moved to St. Catharine's on February 1, 1991. However, in the absence of further activity the case took a back seat and the forensic samples—including those submitted by Bernardo after his interview with the police—were no longer a priority. Of course, just because Bernardo had moved didn't mean he'd reformed. In April of 1991, he committed his 12th rape, his first in St. Catharine's.

By this point, Bernardo had concluded that he could not support his rapacious lifestyle with a regular job. He became a predator on the lookout for an opportunity to strike it rich. In the meantime, he took to smuggling to make ends meet.

Homolka knew exactly what he was up to, but she kept quiet about it. Insecurity about losing him ranked high in her thoughts. She needed a way to bring the romance back into their lives and was ready to do anything to be the perfect girlfriend.

Homolka had become friends with a 15-year-old girl now known as Jane Doe when she worked at a pet store. She invited Jane for a girls' night out on June 7, 1991, and during the course of the evening, she offered the teenager alcohol laced with Halcion (triazolam). She told Bernardo that Jane, who was a look-alike of her dead sister Tammy, was her wedding gift to him. Once Jane lost consciousness, Homolka raped the girl herself while

Bernardo videotaped them. Then he took his turn and entered her both vaginally and anally.

Jane was nauseous the next morning, but she assumed that her vomiting was caused by a hangover from the previous night's drinking. She had no idea that she had been raped.

In August, Homolka invited Jane to spend the night. History repeated itself, and soon Jane stopped breathing due to an overdose. Bernardo went ahead and raped her anyway. Perhaps having learned her lesson after Tammy's death, Homolka called 911 for help but called again a few minutes later saying that Jane had started breathing again and was fine.

Early in the morning on June 15, 1991, Bernardo was in Burlington, midway between St. Catherine's and Toronto, to steal license plates when he noticed 14-year-old Leslie Mahaffy. The rebellious teenager was sitting outside her door after missing her curfew, and the devil within Bernardo resurfaced. Under the pretext of offering her a cigarette, he took her to his car and forced her to get inside. Then he blindfolded her and took her to Port Dalhousie.

There, Bernardo and Homolka raped Leslie and videotaped her as she begged them to stop the unspeakable sexual horrors. At one point the girl made the fatal mistake of telling them that her blindfold was slipping. Worried that she would be able to identify them if she was allowed to live, they killed her. According to Bernardo, Homolka administered a fatal dose of Halcion. Homolka, on the other hand, later claimed that Bernardo strangled her.

They stashed Leslie's body in their basement while Homolka's family joined them for dinner that night, then formulated a grisly plan to get rid of the evidence for good. They tore Leslie limb from limb and enclosed each piece of her in a cement block. They then dumped the blocks in Lake Gibson, 11 miles to the south of Port Dalhousie. Leslie's body was discovered on June 29, 1991—the same day Bernardo and Homolka said 'I Do'.

Homolka was like a possessed soul with no control over her mind. On April 16, 1992, she helped Bernardo kidnap 15-year-old Kristen French as the girl was walking out of Holy Cross School. Homolka strode up to Kristen with a map and asked for directions while Bernardo sneaked up from behind and jostled her. Incredibly, they were able to kidnap her amidst a large crowd of people.

At home, they plied her with large amounts of alcohol while raping her repeatedly. They also showed her the video of Leslie Mahaffy, sensing she would respond more submissively after seeing it. And of course, they made more videos, which showed three days of continual torture during which Bernardo repeatedly threatened to and then actually did urinate on Kristen's face. He also placed his buttocks on her face in an attempt to defecate on her.

Since Kristen had not been blindfolded and would surely be able to recognize her attackers, Bernardo had planned to exterminate her from the beginning. He eventually strangled her with the same cord used to kill Leslie, and once again this barbarous act was followed by dinner with Homolka's family. They later discarded Leslie's body in Burlington, where it was found on April 30, 1992.

It was around this time that Bernardo and Homolka decided to change their names. Bernardo felt no connection with his surname since Kenneth Bernardo was not his biological father, and so they chose a new last name to go with their new marriage: Teale, after serial killer Martin Thiel in the movie

Criminal Law. Bernardo also wanted a new middle name: Jason, from the character in the *Friday the 13th* movies. Their request was approved less than a week before he was arrested.

Each rape added to Bernardo's tally of crimes, which eventually totaled at least 15 violent rapes before and after meeting Homolka. Soon enough, his name resurfaced out of the information that investigators were obtaining from various victims. In late 1992, Bernardo was once again interviewed by two policemen, and once again he was extremely gracious and helpful throughout. He even admitted that he had been a suspect earlier.

The policemen accordingly wrote to Detective Irwin in Toronto to inquire about the test results for the blood samples of the Scarborough Rapist. More than a week later, Detective Irwin replied that the tests on Bernardo's blood and saliva samples had been halted midway through. So, technically, Bernardo was still a suspect.

During this period the police also learned that Bernardo had just been charged with assault in St. Catharine's. The charges, it turned out, had been filed by none other than Karla Homolka.

Good Riddance to Bad Rubbish

Homolka had become yet another victim of Bernardo's wrath in December of 1992 when he beat her black and blue with a flashlight. Following years of suppressed emotions, Homolka went to the police and claimed to be a victim of domestic violence.

Then, in February 1993, the Toronto forensic department finally processed Bernardo's DNA samples 26 months after receiving them. The police were informed that they matched the samples of the Scarborough Rapist. How many innocent lives could have been saved had authorities not been so negligent during the time Bernardo was relatively inactive! In a classic case of shutting the stable door after the horse has bolted, Bernardo was now placed under 24-hour surveillance.

Toronto investigators interviewed Homolka on February 9. Homolka mainly concentrated on how Bernardo had abused her. When she learned that Bernardo had been implicated in the rapes, though, she became fearful of being arrested herself. Two days later she met with lawyer George Walker, who then tried to get her legal immunity in exchange for her cooperation.

But by now the investigation into Tammy Homolka's death had also been reopened, and prosecutors rejected this proposal out of hand. They offered Karla Homolka a choice between twelve years in prison term or trial on three murder charges. She opted for the former and testified against Bernardo in 1995.

Why would prosecutors offer such an attractive deal to a woman who had been so intimately involved in so many rapes and murders? It turns out that Homolka's then-defense lawyer, Ken Murray, kept the videotapes that Bernardo and Homolka made of their crimes hidden for 17 months. Prosecutors stated that they would never have agreed to the plea bargain if they had seen this crucial evidence before. Understandably, the deal came in for considerable public criticism once the tapes were disclosed.

Homolka entered the Prison For Women, located in Kingston, Ontario, in June of 1993 and served all twelve years of her sentence. While she was eligible for parole, she never bothered to apply.

Bernardo's trial for the murders of Kristen French and Leslie Mahaffy took place in 1995. He was charged with first-degree murder, aggravated assault, kidnapping, forcible confinement, and performing an inhuman act on a human body. The evidence against him included videotapes of the rapes and detailed testimony from Homolka.

On September 1, 1995, Bernardo was found guilty of all charges. He was sentenced to life in prison with no chance of parole for 25 years. He was taken to Kingston Penitentiary and confined in a tiny prison cell for 23 hours a day.

In November of 1995, Bernardo was declared a Dangerous Offender for raping 14 women in and around Toronto. This label guaranteed that he would remain behind bars for life.

Homolka has faced a lot of scrutiny following her release from prison on July 4, 2005. She eventually settled in Quebec, where she lives with her new husband and three children. In 2017, it was reported that she had been volunteering at a Montreal elementary school. Enraged local citizens petitioned the school to reconsider its decision.

Bernardo is currently serving a life sentence for the kidnapping, rape, and murder of Leslie Mahaffy and Kristen French.

He technically became eligible for day parole in 2015 and for full parole in February of 2018. However, due to his Dangerous Offender status, it is improbable that he will ever be released from prison.

Clifford Olson
The Beast of British Columbia

Early Years of Life

Clifford Robert Olson Jr. got his first taste of publicity on the day of his birth. It was on the first day of January in the year 1940—New Year's Day. Like other babies born in St. Paul's Hospital in Vancouver on that special day, he received a gift from Cunningham Drug Store. Who was to know that he would grow up to rob that very same store?

Clifford Jr. was the first child of Clifford and Leona Olson. He was raised in a stable home along with three younger siblings, none of whom ever had skirmishes with the law. In 1945, the Olson family moved to British Columbia, where they lived in a community built for war veterans.

As a schoolboy, Clifford Jr. was frequently involved in fights, which he frequently lost. Clifford Sr. recalled him wanting to learn boxing so that he could get even with those who kept beating him up. He ended up becoming fairly good at the sport, even winning a few prizes. Unfortunately, he also used his newfound physical prowess to bully other kids and torment animals. He started skipping classes by the time he turned 10, and he quit school completely in 8th grade to work at a racetrack.

And then he began his life of crime. His first arrest, at the age of 17, was for breaking and entering. He was sent to a correctional center in Burnaby for nine months. He absconded from there but was caught again and sent to the Haney Correctional Institution.

The Beginning of a Criminal Living

For the next quarter century, Olson played a drawn-out game of hide and seek with the police. He amassed nearly 100 convictions for offenses from forgery and fraud to burglary, rape and finally homicide. He managed to escape from prison seven times.

Olson was also a con artist, and many described him as a charming man with the gift of gab. He didn't have a temper, but he was never known to back down from a challenge. When he was in prison, he never hesitated to rat on his fellow inmates if it suited his purpose. Because of this, he was often attacked by other prisoners, and he had to be moved repeatedly from one facility to another to keep him from being murdered.

One such move came after he befriended a prisoner named Gary Marcoux who had brutally raped and murdered a young girl. Olson had extracted the details of the crime from Marcoux, then assisted in convicting his "friend". This episode also led to a new interest for Olson—child pornography. When Olson was released from jail in 1978, he began indulging in child pornography and would doubtless have been arrested for it had he not been arrested on another charge, the rape of a 16-year-old girl, in January of 1981. His lawyer managed to get him out on bail in April because no one realized that he had killed a 12-year-old girl the previous year.

The girl, Christine Weller, had disappeared in November of 1980. As she had run away once before, her family did not report it until more than a week later. Her remains, marred by repeated stabbing, were finally the next month, on Christmas Day.

Olson killed his second victim within eight days of receiving his bail in April of 1981. He convinced the victim, 13-year-old Colleen Daignault, to get into his car with what was to become his regular ploy. He would meet youngsters at video arcades or other places where they hung out. He would even advertise on church bulletin boards. He would hand out professional-looking business cards identifying him as a construction contractor. He would interview some of his marks on the pretext of giving them a job as a window washer or some such and then select a particularly naive one to accompany him to the construction site in his car. En route, he would give them a drink to celebrate. It would be laced with chloral hydrate, a knockout drug. He would then drive to a deserted place where he would rape and murder them.

He used the same ploy on his third victim, Daryn Johnsrude, who was 16 years old when he was murdered on April 21, 1981. With Daryn, however, Olson broke his pattern by opting for a male teenager. This change made it more confusing for investigators, who didn't yet realize that there was a serial killer involved but assumed that the missing teenagers were simply runaways.

Another reason that Olson evaded suspicion at the outset was that the cops thought of him as an informant rather than a suspect. Besides, he had never been accused of any sex crimes before the rape charge in January of 1981, and in that case, the alleged victim was a prostitute who often failed to appear in court and proved to be an unreliable witness when she did. She later retracted her accusation.

While out of jail in 1980, Olson had met a divorcee named Joan Hale. She had suffered through a vicious, abusive marital life, and Olson found it easy to seduce this weak, nervous woman. She gave birth to his son in April of 1981, and the two got married on May 15 of the same year—right in the middle of his murder binge. Olson's new bride had no idea that her husband had killed three children. He led a double life, attending church to show everyone that he was a family man while he made his living as a scam artist and thief.

Four days after the wedding, he picked up his fourth victim, a 16-year-old girl named Sandra Lynn Wolfsteiner, and killed her by repeatedly bludgeoning her head with a hammer. On June 21, 13-year-old Ada Anita Court became his fifth victim when he picked her up as she was returning home from a babysitting job. She was also murdered by multiple hammer blows to the head.

Olson's sixth victim changed the way the authorities treated the cases. Simon Partington disappeared on July 2, 1981. He was only 9 years old, and this convinced investigators that they were not looking at runaways but at something entirely more sinister. But an extraordinarily long time had passed before the cops figured out that the disappearances that had occurred in multiple jurisdictions across a wide area of the Lower Mainland were actually connected.

A Friend or Foe?

While these cases were being analyzed, police had let Olson slip through their fingers not once but twice. A week after Daryn Johnsrude went missing they had arrested Olson on a shoplifting charge. Olson was also charged for an indecent assault on a 16-year-old five days after Simon Partington disappeared, but he was released.

On July 15, Olson's name was mentioned for the first time at a law enforcement conference on the disappearances, and from then on he was treated as a serious suspect. He was subjected to sporadic surveillance, but he still managed to cause four more fatalities in the last weeks of July.

July of 1981 was a busy month for Olson; he murdered six children during that short span of time. After Simon Partington on July 2, his next victim was 14-year-old Judy Kozma, who was slaughtered on the ninth. With this killing, Olson reached new heights in his perversion and actually called the Kozmas' landlord and played a tape recording of Judy's cries of agony. He also made threatening calls to her closest friends warning them that they would be next.

Despite the police surveillance, Olson was able to rape and murder 15-year-old Raymond Lawrence King Jr. on July 23, an 18-year-old German tourist named Sigrun Charlotte Arnd on July 25, 15-year-old Terry Lyn Carson on July 27, and 17-year-old Louise Simmone Marie Evelyn Chartrand on July 30. All of them were strangled, stabbed or clubbed with a hammer or rocks. Some of the bodies were so badly mutilated that it was difficult to identify them. The cops had to use dental records to identify Sigrun Arnd.

By July 28, police were certain that they had found the killer. They set up a meeting with Olson under the pretext that they needed his services as an informant. Olson agreed to assist them. In fact, he seemed eager to help even after he was specifically told that they were looking for leads in the Lower Mainland Missing Children Case. This led investigators to believe that Olson now wanted to be caught. He knew that he was probably under investigation, but he was able to murder Louise Chartrand two days later without being observed.

Olson had rented several cars to carry out his killings, and he owed a lot of money to the car rental companies. Desperate for cash, he broke into at least two homes in early August.

The Arrest

On August 12, 1981, Olson was finally arrested when officers trailed his car to a deserted area after picking up two young girls. They watched him order one girl to get out, then apprehended him as he was making off with the other one. When they searched his car, they found an address book with Judy Kozma's name in it.

Olson was formally charged for the murder of Judy Kozma six days later. The case started with very little physical evidence against him; the diary with Judy Kozma's address written in her own handwriting was all prosecutors had. This wasn't enough to build a case, and while four bodies had now been found, there was no way to link them to Olson. The authorities were desperate to locate the remaining bodies and extract a confession so that the victims' families could be appeased and a murderer could be brought to justice.

Olson offered them a deal: He would plead guilty to 11 killings and take police to the locations where he'd hidden the victims' remains, but in exchange he wanted his wife to receive a sum of $10,000 for each victim. The investigators were initially outraged by this suggestion, but since they still had no concrete evidence against him, they eventually agreed to the deal. They paid Olson's wife a total of $100,000 in exchange for Olson's leading them to 10 murder sites and 10 bodies. (Olson was so thrilled with the deal that he threw in the 11th body as a freebie, he liked to boast.)

The details of this cash-for-bodies deal were only revealed after Olson was sentenced in January of 1982. The families of seven of the children then filed suit demanding that this money be given to them as compensation for the murders. They lost the case, however, as the court ruled that the payment was not made as compensation but had instead been authorized to obtain evidence necessary to convict Olson of the crimes.

Olson's wife, Joan, who had played the role of a dutiful wife all throughout his trial, testified during these hearings that her husband was an alcoholic who frequently beat her and had only married her for the alimony she was receiving following her divorce. She also said that he had confessed to her after his trial, explaining that he couldn't help raping and killing because of "the booze and the pills". Joan went on to divorce him in 1985.

Olson offered the cops one more deal after the 11 bodies were found—a massive cut-price bargain of $100,000 for 20 more bodies. Since Olson was going to prison anyway, the authorities decided not to accept it, so we can only wonder how many more victims are still out there.

In custody, Olson continued to create controversy with ludicrous petitions. He demanded parole hearings on multiple occasions, although all of his bids were rejected. He made media claims about book signings, attempted to escape from prison, and sent revoltingly explicit letters to the families of some of the victims before authorities began screening his mail. Olson never showed any remorse for his monstrous deeds, and every time he appeared in the news, the victims' families felt their pain all over again. But they finally felt at peace when on September 30, 2011, the media reported that Olson had died of cancer at the age of 71.

Cody Legebokoff
The Country Boy Killer

At about 9:45 PM on the 27th of November, 2010, the Royal Canadian Mounted Police stopped a truck that was driving above the speed limit on the highway between Vanderhoof and Fort St. James, British Columbia. The driver was Cody Legebokoff, and he had blood smeared all over his face. In response to the cops' raised eyebrows, he explained that he had been poaching deer with a friend and used a pipe wrench to "put one out of its misery."

Unconvinced, the cops detained him under the Wildlife Act. The conservation officer they brought in discovered not a dead deer but the body of Loren Leslie along a logging road. She was lying in the snow without pants, shoes or underwear, her throat slit, and blood spilling out.

They interrogated Legebokoff and he presented a series of increasingly ridiculous accounts of what exactly had happened to Loren. Basically, he insisted that she killed herself, stating at one point that "she just went fuckin' crazy" and beat herself with a pipe wrench before stabbing herself in the neck. The investigators called his story "outrageous and unbelievable", and Legebokoff eventually confessed to beating the girl "a couple of times" with the wrench and then fleeing from the scene with her backpack as all hell broke loose.

This marked the beginning of a months-long bad trip for Cody Legebokoff as further investigation linked him to three more killings. Forensics matched DNA for Jill Stuchenko, 35, Natasha

Montgomery, 23, and Cynthia Maas, 35, to blood stains found in Legebokoff's apartment. Some of his murder weapons, including an axe, a multipurpose tool, and a pickaxe were also discovered there.

Back to Basics

Date of birth: January 1990
Name: Cody Alan Legebokoff
Tried for: Brutal first-degree murders and rape
Date of crime: October 2009—November 2010
Victims: Jill Stacey Stuchenko, 35, Cynthia Frances Maas, 35 Natasha Lynn Montgomery, 23, Loren Donn Leslie, 15
Location of crime: Prince George and Vanderhoof, British Columbia, Canada
Modus operandi: Blunt trauma on various body parts with massive blood loss
Age at crime: 19
Victim Profile: Women who were completely fine with the idea of accompanying an unknown man to his residence or vehicle to drink and take drugs
Conclusion: Stuchenko, Maas, and Montgomery were sex workers. Legebokoff was a cocaine addict who sourced his drugs from prostitutes.
Current status: Serving life in prison since September 16, 2014. Permission for parole declined.

The impression gathered from interviews with his family, friends and school authorities does not portray Legebokoff as a disreputable man. He was instead an intelligent crowd-pleaser who belonged to a warmhearted family. Unfortunately, sometimes appearances are deceptive!

Baby Faced Bloody Faced

Cody Legebokoff is the youngest of three children; he has an elder brother and a younger sister. He remembers an ideal childhood in a loving family environment. An accident at birth that left permanent nerve damage in one of his arms did not stop him from excelling in sports. He played junior hockey at a competitive level and was also on his school's snowboarding team. He enjoyed growing up in the country and often went hunting and fishing with his family and camping with friends. Schoolboy mischief left him with an insignificant criminal record, but he was never "on the radar" of the local police.

Legebokoff lived in Lethbridge for a short time after he graduated from Fort St. James Secondary School. He then relocated to Prince George, where he lived in an apartment with three female roommates. He worked as a mechanic at a Ford dealership and became a regular on the Canadian social-networking site Nexopia with the username 1CountryBoy.

At 6 feet 2 inches and weighing 220 pounds, Legebokoff had quintessentially Canadian boy-next-door looks. Blessed with a fine charm and a laid-back country attitude, he had a pleasing personality that endeared him to all the girls.

The Murders

October 9, 2009, was the last time anyone ever saw Jill Stuchenko alive. While most Canadians were merrily tucking into their Thanksgiving dinner, Jill was dying a horrendous death. Her body was discovered in a gravel pit on the periphery of Prince George four days later.

A mother of six, Jill worked for an escort service. She had visited an addiction treatment center just days before she was killed. An acquaintance testified that she was frantic to get off crack but kept relapsing every time she tried to quit. Additional witnesses confirmed Legebokoff bought, sold and puffed crack himself.

Jill died of extensive blunt force injuries to the head. Bruises from similar blows were also identified on her forehead, arms, and knees. She had lost so much blood that it was difficult for the forensic team to get a sample for analysis.

The postmortem findings, which included DNA analysis of samples taken from under a fingernail and swabs from her vagina and anus, pointed to an unknown male as the perpetrator. When a DNA sample was acquired from Cody Legebokoff following his capture in November of 2010, it was found to be a match with the Stuchenko samples. DNA in cuttings taken from Legebokoff's bloodstained couch also matched that acquired from what was left of Stuchenko's blood.

On studying the evidence, the jury concluded that Legebokoff had murdered Jill in the basement of his apartment over the Thanksgiving weekend of 2009 while his housemates were away for the holiday. Cody Legebokoff was just 19 at the time of the first killing.

23-year-old Natasha Lynn Montgomery went missing between August 30 and September 1, 2010. She was survived by a son and a daughter. She and their father, her long-time boyfriend Godwin, had split up due to her drug addiction. Even so, they remained in touch, and the children called him every other day.

Although Natasha's body was never discovered, numerous items found in Legebokoff's apartment, including clothes, an axe, a comforter and bed sheets, tested positive for her DNA. After studying the evidence, the jury concluded that Natasha Lynn Montgomery had been brutally slaughtered in Legebokoff's apartment. They also concluded the axe was used, perhaps with other weapons, either to kill her or to dispose of her body.

On October 9, 2010, Cynthia Mass was found dead by two policemen patrolling L.C. Gunn Park. Her pants were rolled down to her knees and her body had been hauled up to a tree line. She had suffered blunt force injuries and penetrating lesions to the chest. She also had several fractured ribs and more fractures in the neck, cheekbone, right wrist, both hands, and two fingers. The medical examiner, Dr. Symes, also noticed five dull impressions on the left and top of her skull.

The investigation led to the seizure of a woman's black sweater from behind the driver's seat of Legebokoff's truck. It contained DNA from both Legebokoff and Cynthia, as did a white sock also found in the truck. Subsequent searches of Legebokoff's apartment resulted in the recovery of a pair of black shoes and a pickaxe, both of which tested positive for both Cynthia's and Legebokoff's DNA. The jury studied the evidence and concluded that Legebokoff had murdered Cynthia with the pickaxe.

Born on January 5, 1995, Loren Leslie grew into a visually impaired 15-year-old who died late in the evening of November 27, 2010.

Her body was found hidden in dense bushes by the side of an old logging road off Highway 27 towards Fort St. James by conservation officer Cameron Hill around midnight of the same night. Her pants were rolled down to her ankles, and her body was positioned in a manner that was awfully similar to how Cynthia's had been discovered roughly six weeks before.

Unlike the other three cases, the Leslie investigation got rolling straightaway. Police had much more detailed information about the circumstances leading to Loren's murder, and furthermore, they already had Legebokoff as a prime suspect.

Loren had died from a combination of blood loss from two stab wounds to her neck and brain injury from a succession of colossal blows to the head causing extensive blunt force trauma. Cody Legebokoff had her blood and DNA on his shirt, shorts, and shoes.

A lot of other evidence was available for this case as well. A chain of email and text communications between Loren and Legebokoff that started on November 1, 2010, threw light on their relationship. Loren's cell phone was found in the pocket of Legebokoff's shorts, where he also had a Leatherman multi-tool stained with her blood. A bloody pipe wrench which tested positive for Loren's DNA was found on the floor of Legebokoff's truck, while her wallet, I.D., and backpack sat on the passenger seat.

The jury took one look at this massive pile of incriminating evidence and concluded that Loren Leslie was murdered with the pipe wrench and the Leatherman tool

The Trial

Amy Voell, a former girlfriend of Legebokoff, testified that she had stayed overnight at his 1400-block Liard Drive apartment three to four times a week. She recalled noticing a bloody handprint on a wall near the front door, as well as red stains on the living room curtains and a carpet at the end of the hallway. There was blood on the couch, too, but Amy didn't emphasize this.

When she asked Legebokoff about all these sanguinary stains, he told her that it was his own blood. He'd made a mess of himself while he was high, and he'd gotten a nosebleed which accounted for the blood on the curtain.

Amy told authorities that they'd both had work that day, but Legebokoff's shift had ended before hers. When Amy got off she made the brief drive to Legebokoff's apartment, where they relaxed and watched TV. She left at around 6:30 because Legebokoff was feeling extremely sleepy, and that was the last she saw of him.

On August 26 and 27, 2014, Legebokoff took the witness stand and informed the jury of the existence of three individuals he identified as X, Y and Z who he claimed had played a comprehensive role in the murders of Jill Stuchenko, Cynthia Maas, and Natasha Montgomery. (It would have been too unbelievable to try to pin the murder of Loren Leslie on them as well, so he didn't even try.) During his testimony, Legebokoff flat-out announced that he wouldn't be telling the whole truth because he wasn't going to tell the court who X, Y, and Z were.

As per Legebokoff, he routinely met drug dealer X from the end of August until October 10, 2009, roughly six weeks. X had gotten acquainted with Legebokoff and trusted him enough to bring his victims to Legebokoff's residence to kill them. X mistakenly believed that Legebokoff would take part in the killings. While Legebokoff testified that he hadn't done that, he had nonetheless been a fairly accommodating host. Not only did he allow the murders to take place in his residence, he even provided the tools. Cynthia, however, had not been killed by X in Legebokoff's apartment but by Y in L.C. Gunn Park—with the pickaxe that Legebokoff provided.

The only problem with Legebokoff's story was that there was not a shred of independent evidence that X, Y, and Z actually existed. It seemed that the terrible trio had blown through the crime scenes without leaving so much as a drop of DNA evidence—neither on clothing, nor on the murder weapons, nor on the two bodies that were recovered. The jury concluded that these nameless and faceless individuals were invented by Legebokoff from whole cloth.

Furthermore, Legebokoff stated that X, Y, and Z each committed a single one of the murders. This seemed especially odd since they had apparently all been present at all of the murders. But a close examination of Legebokoff's testimony showed that at no point in time did more than one person attack any of the victims. For example, Legebokoff had stated that he and Y just sat around while X attacked the victims and also wrestled with Natasha for approximately five minutes.

Finally, on September 16, 2014, Cody Legebokoff was sentenced to life in prison with no parole for 25 years.

Allan Joseph Legere
The Monster of the Miramichi

Allan Joseph Legere is a Canadian serial killer and arsonist. He was nicknamed the Monster of the Miramichi due to the fear he instilled in the hearts of the inhabitants of the Miramichi River valley of New Brunswick in 1989. Legere was found guilty of a murder binge that included the torture, rape, and slaying of three women and the killing of an old Catholic priest.

On May 3 of that year, at 10:40 AM, Legere, already a convicted killer, absconded from a restroom at the Dr. Georges L. Dumont Hospital in Moncton. He was serving a life sentence at the Atlantic Institution, a maximum security prison in Renous, for the ruthless killing of convenience store owner John Glendenning but had developed an ear infection and been escorted to the hospital for treatment. Once at the hospital, Legere, in handcuffs and leg shackles, asked to use the restroom. After a few minutes, he opened the door a little and asked for some toilet paper. While the guard was distracted, Legere burst out and made his escape. He left the cuffs and the shackles behind in the sink.

Legere went into hiding while the cops hunted for him, but that doesn't mean he kept his head down. He remained a fugitive for seven exceptionally gory months over which he murdered four people and sexually assaulted a fifth before leaving her to die. His victims included an elderly store owner called Annie Flam; two middle-aged sisters, Donna and Linda Daughney; and an elderly priest, Father James Smith.

The sheer cruelty, barbarism and inhumanity of their deaths traumatized and petrified Miramichi residents, and the fright and panic percolated throughout the province. With this murderer out on the run, New Brunswickers were afraid and cautious. Children weren't permitted to play outdoors by themselves, and people kept guns and other weapons handy.

Legere's escape and the ensuing murders triggered one of the biggest manhunts in the history of the Royal Canadian Mounted Police. The case also publicized the then-new science of DNA analysis. While DNA analysis has now become a routine and familiar investigative tool, Legere was the first Canadian ever to be convicted of murder through this technique—fortunately enough, because there were no eyewitnesses to the killings he committed.

With his third murder, Legere earned the terrible title of serial killer. Once he was caught, tried, sentenced, and locked away for life in prison, the people of Miramichi could finally breathe easy again. They and their loved ones were out of danger.

Early Life, First Murder, and Escape

Allan Joseph Legere was born on February 13, 1948, in Chatham, New Brunswick. In the late 1970s, he worked as a car salesman in Winchester, south of Ottawa, and lived in a farmhouse in nearby Inkerman. Later, he returned to his New Brunswick birthplace—and that's when his name became tantamount to terror.

On June 21, 1986, Legere and a couple of collaborators, Todd Matchett and Scott Curtis, cut the power and broke into an aged couple's store in Black River Bridge. They beat the elderly shopkeeper John Glendenning and his wife Mary severely and then bolted from the scene. When Mary regained consciousness, she found that her spouse had been beaten to death. She called 911 and the dispatcher stayed on the line with her until emergency responders reached the scene. The police quickly hunted down the three attackers and arrested them. Matchett pleaded guilty to the murder of John Glendenning, while Legere and Curtis were found guilty at trial.

Legere was incarcerated at the Atlantic Institution maximum security prison in Renous-Quarryville, managed by the Correctional Service of Canada (CSC). In the spring of 1989 he developed an ear infection that needed medical attention, and on May 3rd, CSC personnel took Legere from the prison to Dr. Georges L. Dumont Regional Hospital in Moncton, about 75 miles to the south. He was transported in handcuffs, a body chain, and leg shackles.

At the hospital, Legere persuaded the CSC guard to let him use the restroom unaccompanied. Once he was alone, he picked the locks on his restraints with a handmade key that he had concealed in a cigar. He then burst out of the bathroom and used a TV antenna that he had hidden on his body to fend off the guards as he escaped from the building. Legere ran away from the area on foot and then committed a series of carjackings and car thefts to avoid recapture.

More Murders and Eventual Capture

For seven months, Legere played the role of an escaped convict to a T. No laying low or hiding in a basement for him—he spent his time committing four more murders, along with arson and multiple rapes. The gruesome sex slaughters took place in and around the towns of Chatham, New Castle, and the adjoining areas which are now part of the city of Miramichi. This seven-month period was known as the "Reign of Terror" in Miramichi.

Legere first murdered 75-year-old Annie Flam, a Chatham store owner, on May 29, 1989, 25 days after he escaped. He killed her in her home and assaulted her sister at the same time.

His next victims were sisters Linda and Donna Daughney, aged 45 and 41 respectively, on October 13, 1989. Legere murdered them in their Newcastle home and then set fire to it before he left.

On November 16, 1989, Legere killed his final victim, 69-year-old Catholic priest James Smith, in his Chatham Head rectory.

The sympathetic nature of his victims contrasted sharply with the savagery of Legere's assaults. According to New Brunswick Court of Appeal Justice Lewis Ayles, he spent hours tormenting the four before they finally passed away.

On November 24, 1989, Legere was finally apprehended on Route 118 while trying to make his way back to Miramichi after a series of botched carjackings that started in Saint John and finished outside Rogersville. The previous 201 days had seen one of the largest manhunts in Canadian history, and $50,000 in reward money was handed out for the information that resulted in his arrest.

Conviction

In August of 1990, Legere was sentenced to nine years upon conviction of charges connected to his escape. His murder trial, which began in November, marked the first time in Canadian legal history that DNA evidence was used to convict rather than acquit. Although his lawyers argued that the comparatively shallow gene pool of the Miramichi region could easily lead to false positives, the jury wasn't persuaded.

It took less than a month for these six women and five men to find Legere guilty on four counts of murder. When they announced the verdict, Justice David Dickson told them, "I don't usually comment on verdicts… But let me say this: Don't lose too much sleep over your verdict."

Legere was sent to the special handling unit (SHU) at Sainte-Anne-des-Plaines Institution near Montreal, a maximum security facility that houses some of Canada's most dangerous offenders. He was one of only 90 inmates, and he was shunned by the other prisoners there because they detested his crimes against women and children.

Reign of Terror

Legere's crime spree after his escape generated a wave of terror in the Miramichi area. Those who lived by themselves moved in with friends or family for security. Gun sales skyrocketed. Few people went out after dark, and Halloween trick-or-treating was called off that year.

In 2014, the 25th anniversary of Legere's capture, people from the communities that he terrified still remembered everything that had transpired, but most chose not to fixate on it.

"It's something we'll never forget," said Miramichi Police veteran Sgt. Bob Bruce, who was a part of the 1989 manhunt for Legere. "It's part of our history, not something we're proud of but we survived and moved on from it. I didn't really realize it was that long ago. Some of it feels like yesterday."

"They were certainly dark days," says Miramichi Police Chief Paul Fiander. "People were paranoid and rightfully so."

Bruce said there was a constructive and encouraging transformation among citizens along the Miramichi resulting from Legere's capture that he still perceives 25 years later. "You can't drive down the street here; you almost wear your arm out as a police officer waving because everybody waves to you. It is a great community—there's a sense of community. People look out for each other."

"It doesn't seem like 25 years have gone by," said Lise Black, who in 1989 had only just relocated to the region as a young newlywed. "I used to be so scared. I remember my husband would leave for work and I would lock the doors all day and never go out."

"It was a bad scene, really," said Bryce Silliker, 35, captain of Miramichi's senior hockey team, the Phantoms, who was only 10 years old at the time. "It's hard to forget, but we move on the best we can and everyone bonded together and the community stayed strong."

Phantoms head coach David Morrison, 39, was just a little older than Silliker when the killings occurred. He felt that connections among the neighbors around the river most certainly grew stronger after the tragedy. "I was 14 at the time. I remember not being able to leave the house and having an aluminum baseball bat under my bed," Morrison said. "I remember terror in the whole city. You know, we try and forget it and try and put it in our past, but it's something that's always there."

Still, he said residents would not allow the happenings of 1989 define the region. "I wouldn't want to live anywhere else. The people are supportive. It's a small community and everyone knows each other. It's where I'm from and where I want to be."

Present

The city of Fredericton closed its old jail in 1996 and converted the building into a science museum in 1999. The cell where Legere was locked up for the duration of his trial in 1991 is currently used for a display on DNA fingerprinting.

Legere, who is now 70, has been declared a Dangerous Offender, a label that permits permanent imprisonment.

In 2015, Legere was relocated from the maximum security prison in Sainte-Anne-des-Plaines, Quebec, to the Edmonton Institution in Alberta.

The deputy mayor of Miramichi and former New Brunswick public safety minister, John Foran, spoke about apprehensions related to the relocation of Legere to a lower-security facility and the threat of escape.

"He could escape any institution, I think, if the opportunity comes along, and I'm sure for the last 25 years that's where his mind has been all the time, trying to connive and think of some way that if he ever gets the opportunity how he would go about doing it."

Even though the Edmonton facility is farther away, Foran had concerns that Legere would use the relocation "as some kind of a method to get transferred back to the Miramichi area at the Atlantic Institution," as he has requested previously, and would eventually escape.

Foran feared that Legere's new jailers wouldn't realize what he was capable of. "I really believe that the opportunity could be there for him to escape. And a lot of those officers, I feel, would not look at him the same as the ones who were there 25 years ago. If they're between, say 25 and 35, they wouldn't know who he was or remember what he did."

Gilbert Paul Jordan
The Boozing Barber

We have all heard of serial killers, and many of us are aware of their most common methods of murder. Some of them strangle their victims, some stab them, and others bludgeon them with blunt objects. But credit for one of the most creative and least suspicious techniques goes to Gilbert Paul Jordan, AKA the Boozing Barber. Jordan got his victims so drunk they were almost comatose and then killed them by forcing them to drink even more.

Jordan was connected to the deaths of eight to ten women in Vancouver, British Columbia, from 1965 to 1988, and may have been involved in dozens of more deaths which could not be directly linked to him. He was the first Canadian known to have used alcohol as a murder weapon. He was also a severe alcoholic himself and frequently paid Native prostitutes in Vancouver's Downtown Eastside to have a few—well, many—drinks with him. Once they blacked out, Jordan would continue pouring vodka or some other liquor down their throats until they died.

His extensive criminal record included sentences for crimes as varied as rape, indecent assault, drunk driving, hit-and-run and car theft. These preceded his arrest for the "alcohol murders" for which he served six years for manslaughter.

When Dr. Tibor Bezeredi conducted a court-ordered psychological examination of Jordan in 1976, he diagnosed him with an antisocial personality disorder. Dr. Bezeredi explained that was Jordan "a person whose conduct is maladjusted in terms of social behavior; disregard for the rights of others which often results in unlawful activities".

Jordan died in 2006.

Early Life

Jordan was born in Vancouver on December 12, 1931. His name at birth was Gilbert Paul Elsie. By the time he reached the age of 16, he had become an alcoholic and dropped out of high school. By the time he was 21, he had an extensive criminal record covering a multitude of crimes such as rape, assault, theft, and possession of heroin.

Jordan had an insatiable appetite for liquor and drunken sex. He was an uncontrolled alcoholic who regularly consumed over three pints of vodka a day. He sought out the company of other alcoholics as a matter of necessity. As he explained during the course of his trial, "I didn't want to drink in my room all by myself," and sober people wouldn't have anything to do with him, so he had no choice but to hang out with other alcoholics.

He also claimed that he had sex with over 200 women a year. He hunted for prostitutes in the slums, low-end bars and seediest dives of Vancouver.

Jordan was often found on the wrong side of the law. In 1961, he was caught with a five-year-old Aboriginal girl in his car and charged with kidnapping. However, the case came to a standstill with a stay in proceedings in May of 1961 and he was never convicted.

Shortly after Christmas in the same year, Jordan threatened to jump off the Lions Gate Bridge in a drunken stupor. Traffic came to a halt until he was coaxed into backing off. Not much later, he was reprimanded for contempt of court when he gave a Nazi-style salute in a North Vancouver courtroom.

In 1963, Jordan invited two women to drink with him in his car. Once they were drunk, he raped them and stole their belongings. He was charged with rape and theft, but although he was convicted of the theft, he was cleared of the rape charge due to lack of evidence.

Jordan continued to sexually assault helpless women on a regular basis, and this led to him being in and out of jail on a regular basis. He learned the barber's trade during one of his many stints in prison, and when he got out he started running the Slocan Barber Shop on Kingsway Avenue in Vancouver's seedy Downtown Eastside. He also inherited some money and invested it in the stock market.

Soon, the Boozing Barber added murder to his already long list of crimes. His investments had paid off. He could afford a good lawyer.

Killings

Jordan's first victim was English-born, but all of his other victims were Native women from the infamous Downtown Eastside. His modus operandi was to stalk Native American prostitutes in seedy joints. He would offer the women cash for sex and company and take them to his ramshackle barber shop or a cheap hotel room. He would encourage them to drink with him and would offer more money if they could consume straight liquor. When they blacked out, he would pour more liquor down their throats and rape them as they breathed their last.

Jordan, being a heavy drinker, blended in well with the locals at the bars he frequented. With a bald head, thick black-rimmed glasses and a short and stocky physique, he came across as a milquetoast compared to the burnt-out junkies and prostitutes swarming around him. Nobody would ever look at him and think he was dangerous, so it was relatively easy for him to lure women who seemed to be "on their last legs". These women were alcoholics like him and did not mix with the drug crowd. They appreciated free drinks and they readily went along with Jordan's propositions.

Jordan was just as indiscriminate in his choice of companions. During a deposition, he stated that "I didn't give a damn who I was with. I mean, we're all dying sooner or later, whether it's in this bar, across the street, or wherever."

Despite his lowlife lifestyle, Jordan had received a sizeable inheritance and made wise investments whose good returns enabled him to hire the best lawyers. And despite his numerous crimes, this kept him from being declared a Dangerous Offender for many years. But it all changed when the rapes and assaults turned into murders.

Ivy Rose (Doreen) Oswald, a switchboard operator, joined Jordan on one of his drinking sprees one night in 1965. Her naked body was discovered in a Vancouver hotel room the next day. Her blood alcohol level was found to be 0.51.

The legal driving limit is 0.08 in most countries, and death by alcohol poisoning usually occurs at a level of approximately 0.4. Guzzling a dozen beers would result in a blood alcohol level of approximately 0.3, at which point the drinker would probably pass out. For alcohol poisoning to result in death, the drinker would have to drink an enormous quantity of alcohol extremely quickly.

Still, Doreen's death was deemed accidental, and the case was closed. Her murderer confessed to the crime over 22 years later.

Subsequent Charges and Convictions

Soon after his first murder, Gilbert Paul Elsie filed an application to change his surname to Jordan. The request was granted.

Jordan continued to amass more charges and convictions under his new name, including many for drunk driving. In 1969 he was even charged twice in one day. Other criminal charges during this period included:

- Committing an indecent act in a public place (1971, Vancouver)
- Indecent exposure (1973, Mackenzie)
- Indecent assault (1974, Prince George)

He was convicted on the 1974 charge and served a sentence of nearly two years. By now, the Crown was trying hard to get Jordan declared a Dangerous Offender, but his lawyers still managed to get the request denied.

As soon as he got out of prison in 1975, he went back to his old ways and then some. Feeling not the slightest guilt or remorse, that very same year he abducted a mentally impaired woman from a mental institute and raped her. If the court needed evidence that Jordan was a dangerous sex offender, here it was. Even without his other crimes, this by itself should have been reason enough to lock him up and throw away the key.

This revolting act garnered him several charges, including kidnapping and sexual intercourse with a frail-minded person. However, the court did not take his previous convictions into account and dealt with him with more leniency than he deserved. He received a sentence of only 26 months for this horrendous crime—and that had disastrous ramifications when he was released from prison and went on a killing binge that claimed the lives of several more women.

Between July of 1982 and June of 1985, three women died at Slocan Barber Shop on Kingsway Avenue. Jordan, after consulting with his lawyer, reported each of these cases, but he was not investigated. In each case, the coroner reported that the woman had died of alcohol poisoning, and since they were all known alcoholics they were at high risk of just such a fate. Add to that the fact that all three were prostitutes, and it becomes easy to understand why the police paid such little attention to their deaths.

Besides these three, Jordan was also linked to the deaths of three Aboriginal women who were found dead in various hotel rooms. In total, Jordan had been with six women at the time of their deaths:

- On November 30, 1980, Mary Johnson at the Aylmer Hotel with a Blood Alcohol Level of 0.34
- On September 11, 1981, Barbara Paul at the Glenaird Hotel with a Blood Alcohol Level of 0.41
- On July 30, 1982, Mary Johns at Slocan Barbershop with a Blood Alcohol Level of 0.76
- On December 15, 1984, Patricia Thomas at Slocan Barbershop with a Blood Alcohol Level of 0.51
- On June 28, 1985, Patricia Andrew at Slocan Barbershop with a Blood Alcohol Level of 0.79
- On November 19, 1986, Vera Harry at the Clifton Hotel with a Blood Alcohol Level of 0.04

Final Victims

Jordan finally popped up on police radar in 1987. On October 11 he spent the night at the seedy Niagara hotel drinking with a woman later identified as 27-year-old Vanessa Lee Buckner. Jordan left the room many times to buy more alcohol, then left for the last time at around six o'clock on the morning of October 12. At 7:40 AM police received an anonymous phone tip, and when they arrived at the Niagara Hotel they found Vanessa's naked dead body.

Vanessa was an occasional prostitute and a moderate drinker, but her Blood Alcohol Level was 0.91, more than 11 times the legal limit for driving and more than twice the amount needed to kill a person. During the trial, it was revealed that Jordan had poisoned her and raped her. Then, as a black liquid began to ooze from her mouth and nose, he absconded from the room and left her alone to die.

Vanessa had recently had a baby, and her father, Nick Basaraba, bitterly expressed his feelings of rage towards Jordan when the case went to trial. "He poisons them and then has sex with them. No parent should have to go through this. He's a worm. He's a lowlife. He should be squashed, just as he squashed a lot of girls' lives."

Police tracked the anonymous early morning phone call to Jordon's room at a nearby hotel, and Jordan's fingerprints were found in the room with Vanessa's body. But although he was questioned about the incident, Jordan was not initially charged with any crime related to this death.

However, a month after Vanessa's murder, another woman was found dead in another hotel. Edna Shade had also died of alcohol poisoning, and once again Jordan's fingerprints were found at the scene. Police then realized that Jordan was the common factor in many similar deaths and put him under surveillance.

In the period between October 12 and November 26, 1987, police watched as Jordan hunted for Native women in Downtown Eastside. On four separate occasions, they rescued women whom Jordan had taken to hotel rooms to indulge in drinking sprees. As they listened outside the doors of those seedy hotel rooms, they heard Jordan say things like:

"Have a drink, down the hatch baby, 20 bucks if you drink it right down; see if you're a real woman; finish that drink, finish that drink, down the hatch hurry, right down; you need another drink, I'll give you 50 bucks if you can take it; I'll give you 10, 20, 50 dollars, whatever you want, come on I want to see you get it all down; you get it right down, I'll give you 50 bucks. I told you that. If you finish that I'll give you $75; finish your drink, I'll give you $20."

Each time, the police intervened and saved the potential victims. The women rescued were:

- On November 20, 1987, Rosemary Wilson at the Balmoral Hotel with a Blood Alcohol Level of 0.52
- On November 21, 1987, Verna Chartrand at the Pacific Hotel with a Blood Alcohol Level of 0.43
- On November 25, 1987, Sheila Joe at the Rainbow Hotel with an unknown Blood Alcohol Level
- On November 26, 1987, Mabel Olson at the Pacific Hotel with an unknown Blood Alcohol Level

The Boozing Barber was finally arrested as he was poisoning his last victim. When police broke into the room she had blacked out and Jordan was sitting astride her, forcing vodka down her throat.

In the end, Gilbert Paul Jordan was linked to at least ten deaths. He was charged for seven of these, but convicted only in the death of Vanessa Lee Buckner. He was sentenced to fifteen years for manslaughter. His lawyers, however, succeeded in reducing his sentence to nine years on appeal.

In reducing the sentence, Justice Sam Toy wrote:

"Although the appellant has left a trail of seven victims, the last was the first occasion when persons in authority, in a forceful and realistic manner, brought to the appellant's attention the fact that supplying substantial quantities of liquor to women who were prepared to drink with him was a contributing cause of their deaths, for which he might be held criminally responsible."

Jordan ended up serving only six of those nine years—less than a year for each woman he killed. Women's groups found this to be a grave insult, and it is most definitely a long way from true justice.

Final Years

In the year 2000, Jordan tried to change his name to Paul Pearce. A name change in British Columbia didn't mandate fingerprinting or a criminal check when he filed the request, but authorities quickly closed this loophole and Jordan withdrew his application forthwith.

In 2002, Jordan was arrested for breaching the terms of his probation. He was found guilty and sentenced to 15 months in prison.

In 2004, the now 72-year-old Jordan was again a free man. He violated his parole straightaway and was re-arrested at a hotel in Winnipeg, Manitoba. Upon his next release in 2005, police issued a public warning:

JORDAN, Gilbert Paul, age 73, is the subject of this alert. JORDAN is 175cm (5'9") tall and weighs 79kgs (174lbs) [sic]. He is partially bald with grey hair and a grey goatee. He has blue eyes and wears glasses. JORDAN is currently in the Victoria area but has no fixed address. JORDAN has a significant criminal record including manslaughter and indecent assault of a female. He uses alcohol to lure his victims. JORDAN's target victim group is adult females. JORDAN is subject to court-ordered conditions including:

- Abstain absolutely from the consumption of alcohol.
- Not to be in the company of any female person or persons in any place where alcohol is being either consumed or possessed by that person or persons.
If you observe the subject in violation of any of the above conditions please call the Saanich Police Department at 475-4321, 911 or your local police agency. If you have questions

concerning the public notification process please contact the BC Corrections Branch at 250-387-6366.

Jordan spent the next two years in and out of prison for parole violations. On July 7, 2006, Gilbert Paul Jordan died in Victoria, British Columbia. The Boozing Barber would booze—and kill—no more.

Canada's Most Notorious Serial Killers

Canada has always been a land of contrast, with dense centers of modern industry coupled with a vast expense of barren waste in the northernmost reaches. It's no coincidence that most of the country's urban population centers are along its southern border: Although Canada's total landmass is tremendous, about 90% of it is completely uninhabitable tundra.

Only the bravest of souls live in the far north, and for most Canadians, their nation runs along a narrow habitable zone from Vancouver in the west to Montreal in the east. This belt is highly urbanized, but a trip a few miles north can take you to virtually uninhabited wilderness. Perhaps it is this vast, cold North that allows so many killers to flourish in Canada. Many of them, like Robert Pickton, have hunted their prey in the big cities and then retreated to isolated lairs in the freezing wasteland.

McArthur, too, is alleged to have picked up his victims in the urban jungle of Toronto's Gay Village before hiding their dismembered corpses all over the countryside of the great Canadian frontier. And then you have Russell Williams, no less than a Colonel in the Canadian Forces, teaching cadets how to save lives by day while he worked hard to take lives by night. Canada's most notorious serial killers come in all shapes and sizes.

Further Readings

As we bring this book to a close we would like to take a moment to acknowledge and introduce to you some of the resources that helped make it possible. Here you will find an overview of every site, newspaper, book, podcast, and blog that helped piece together the complex narratives of the two convicted killers Robert Pickton and Russell Williams, as well as the alleged serial killer Bruce McArthur. Feel free to go through them all for yourself to find out more.

***On the Farm: Robert Pickton and the Tragic Story of Vancouver's Missing Women.* Stevie Cameron**
This book is already a classic, written by a seasoned veteran in the genre of True Crime. It provides an excellent source of information when it comes to Pickton's personal biography, following his life on the farm from beginning to end. Stevie Cameron is an expert in the field, and this book leaves no stone unturned in order to find out what really happened to Vancouver's missing women.

On the Farm is also rather refreshing in the sense that it shines as much of a spotlight on the murder victims as it does on the murderer. If you would like to know more about the lives of those forever lost to us through the callous crimes of Robert Pickton, this book goes the extra mile to provide you with that information.

***Robert Pickton: The Pig Farmer Killer.* Chris Swinney**
While not quite as in-depth as Stevie Cameron's book, *The Pig Farm Killer* does provide some rather interesting angles on the case. It is particularly informative about some of the earlier incidents that are said to have taken place on Pickton's farm. It also provides good insights into the forces that shaped Pickton's

childhood and made him into the monster that he turned out to be.

Butcher. Gary C. King
Another good book on Pickton. This one is a little on the gory side, however, so I don't recommend reading it unless you have a strong stomach. Overall, though, King does a great job of portraying events as they happened.

A New Kind of Monster: The Secret Life and Chilling Crimes of Colonel Russell Williams. Timothy Appleby
Timothy Appleby does such a good job of relating Russell William's life and crimes you would think that he must have gone around recording it on video. But then again—maybe he didn't have to. It is well known that Williams took photos and videos to document his depravity. And while these disturbing images are not available to the general public, there are circumstances when the publication ban can be temporarily lifted.

Perhaps Appleby was one of the few to get through that embargo because the details he provides of the Colonel's diabolical escapades are crystal clear. So, if you think you can stomach it, this book provides an unparalleled perspective on the case of Colonel Russell Williams. Timothy Appleby narrates in dramatic detail from firsthand accounts what went on during Williams's nocturnal trespasses.

www.time.com
Many tidbits of information have been pulled from this site. *Time* does a great job of keeping up to date on unfolding events, such as the ongoing case of Bruce McArthur. Feel free to go online and browse through this resourceful magazine site for yourself.

The Toronto Star
Simply the best newspaper in Canada. You can't find another newspaper with more comprehensive data. Even if you aren't a subscriber, the site allows you to view 10 separate articles before buying a membership, so it's an easy resource to take advantage of.

New York Post
The *New York Post* provides a good rundown of the cases presented in this book, as well as some rare insights that you might not find in other sources—for example, the strange similarities between the alleged landscaping serial killer Bruce McArthur and the Stephen King novel Lawnmower Man. The *New York Post* is full of such unusual anecdotes.

www.cnn.com
You can find a treasure trove of data at CNN. Many may have an axe to grind with this site over claims of media bias, but as far as I can tell—at least as it pertains to suspected serial killers—they remain pleasantly neutral.

Also by Jack Smith

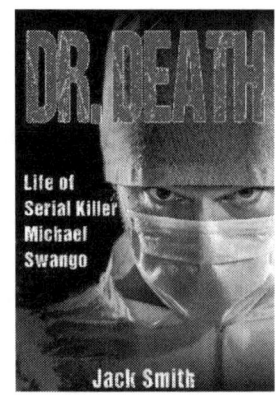

Manufactured by Amazon.ca
Bolton, ON